LAWSUITS

THE WORLD OF CIVIL LITIGATION

THOMAS B. SWANSON, B.A., J.D.

Book and Cover
Design, Concept and Publishing
by Innovative Solutions IT
www.isitonline.com | 281-236-5877

ISBN: 1536912379
ISBN-13: 9781536912371

ABOUT THIS BOOK

This is a book about the mechanics of civil litigation, which is better known to the public as lawsuits. This book explains how lawsuits are constructed and developed for trial. It includes references to both state and federal civil litigation practice. The state that is used as an example in this book is Texas because it has retained many of the traditional common law features that are still used in many states. The federal system is referenced in the book because – well – it is the federal system. Further, it is useful to note that many states borrow heavily from the federal system.

While there are some variations in civil litigation systems in the United States, there are far more similarities. The specialized terminology used in civil litigation and the pre-trial development of lawsuits are very similar throughout the United States.

There are two important sources of law that you will consistently encounter if you work with lawsuits in Texas. They are:
- Rules of Civil Procedure
- Rules of Evidence

Each State has its own rules of civil procedure and evidence. There is access to these laws on the internet. In this book there will be reference to the Texas Rules of Civil Procedure (TRCP) and the Federal Rules of Civil Procedure (FRCP).

In addition to the law referred to above, many trial courts have local rules and these rules may usually be obtained by visiting the web sites of the trial court in question or the clerk of the court.

The book is divided into short, easy to read segments. There is a reason for this approach. Law books in general, and law books on procedure in particular, can induce unintended states of sleep upon the reader. I cringe at the thought of someone being found in a comatose state, holding one of my books. My solution was to organize the book into segments that could be easily and comfortably read in a short period of time. Having educated and trained hundreds of people in civil litigation for over twenty-five years, I have found that such an approach maximizes understanding of the subject matter.

ABOUT THIS BOOK

Finally, please note that this book is not intended as legal advice and is not designed to serve as a substitute for competent legal representation.

THOMAS B. SWANSON
Houston, Texas
July 15, 2016

TABLE OF CONTENTS

LAWSUITS
THE WORLD OF CIVIL LITIGATION

TABLE OF CONTENTS (PAGE 2)

SUBSTANTIVE LAW / PROCEDURAL LAW

Substantive Law defines the rights and duties of people. For example, **contracts** is a category of substantive law that defines the rights and duties of people with respect to the agreements they make. Virtually all substantive law comes from three sources: constitutions, statutes and common law.

Procedural Law is that law used to enforce substantive rights in court. There are three categories of procedural law: rules of procedure, rules of evidence and rules of court (also called "local rules"). Procedural law may be in the form of court rules, statutes or both. **Rules of Procedure** deal with the processing of cases though the trial and appeal courts. Each state court system and the federal court system have rules of procedure. The major purposes of rules of procedure are:

> (1) to provide citizens with due process of law – in other words, fair notice of criminal charges or lawsuits and the opportunity to be heard;

> (2) to permit efficient operation of a court system.

Rules of Evidence determine what information may be considered by a judge or jury in deciding a case. The term **evidence** means that information which may tend to prove or disprove something. Again, each court system has rules of evidence. The purpose of rules of evidence is to insure that the information presented in a case has some minimum degree of reliability. **Rules of Court**, also known as **Local Rules**, are the housekeeping rules of a particular judge or group of judges. For example, one judge may hear presentations on motions on Monday, while another judge may hear presentations on Friday.

Normally, procedural law is not subject to the rule against ex post facto laws. For example, virtually all new laws passed by a legislature cannot be applied retroactively because of the provision in the United States Constitution prohibiting ex post facto laws. However, since procedural law does not define rights or duties, it can often be applied retroactively.

THE LAWSUIT CHECKLIST

Introduction

The following are some important basic terms that you need to know at this point:

- Lawsuit – a request to a court for some form of civil relief.

- Plaintiff (or Petitioner) – one who sues.

- Defendant (or Respondent) – one who is sued.

Recently, legislatures and court systems throughout the United States have expressed concerns about the filing of frivolous lawsuits, meaning lawsuits for which there is no basis in law or fact. The legitimacy of these concerns is subject to debate, as lawsuits have existed for over a thousand years and serve to prevent violence, feuds, vendettas and other breaches of the peace. Nevertheless, there is a small percentage of frivolous lawsuits that are filed and they amount to an abuse of the system. Typically, there are mechanisms to quickly dispose of such lawsuits and often the courts are empowered to sanction those who bring such suits.

The checklist that follows is designed to avoid frivolous lawsuits by setting forth matters that should be considered before filing a lawsuit.

THE SEVEN STEPS OF THE LAWSUIT CHECKLIST

Step One: Establish a set of facts.

Sources:
- a.   client interview
- b.   documents furnished by client
- c.   witness interviews (obtain affidavits if possible)
- d.   investigation
  - public records
  - internet sources
  - private investigators

Sometimes, a complete set of facts cannot be established, even after a good-faith effort, because certain information is not available. If such is the case, it then must be determined whether the facts established are sufficient to permit the filing of a lawsuit.

If not, it may be necessary to seek court assistance in taking a pre-suit deposition to further develop the facts.

Step Two: Determine Cause(s) of Action

A cause of action refers to a legal claim that may be asserted in court based upon a particular set of facts. A particular set of facts may support more than one cause of action and, normally, a party is permitted to assert multiple causes of action in a single lawsuit if supported by the law and the facts. Whether or not a particular set of facts gives rise to a cause or causes of action is normally determined by legal research.

Step Three: Determine the Appropriate Remedies

A remedy is a type of relief that may be granted by a court. The most common remedy is damages, which is a remedy in the form of money. However, depending upon the cause of action asserted, there are a variety of different remedies that may be sought. Remedies will be further discussed in another section.

Step Four: Determine the Appropriate Court(s) Where the Lawsuit May Properly Be Filed (Jurisdiction)

Jurisdiction refers to the authority of a court to hear a case. Normally, there are two types of jurisdiction that a court must have to hear a case:

1.   Subject Matter Jurisdiction = the authority of a court to hear a particular type of case. For example, in Texas, the Justice Court has subject matter jurisdiction over eviction cases; and

2.   Personal (in personam) Jurisdiction = the authority of a court over the parties to a case. Normally, the personal jurisdiction of a state court does not extend beyond the geographical boundaries of the state. Therefore, under most circumstances, a Texas state court would not have personal jurisdiction over persons residing outside the state. One exception to this rule is called long arm jurisdiction, which refers to situations in which a state court has personal jurisdiction over out-of-state residents. Such extended personal jurisdiction is permitted when an out-of-state resident commits misconduct within the state or otherwise has such significant contacts within the state as to render the defendant subject to its jurisdiction. In Texas, long arm jurisdiction is set forth in the Texas Civil Practice and Remedies Code.

Federal Jurisdiction

There are three types of federal civil subject matter jurisdiction:

1. Federal Question Jurisdiction = lawsuits involving federal law;

2. Diversity of Citizenship Jurisdiction = certain lawsuits between residents of different states; andIf not, it may be necessary to seek court assistance in taking a pre-suit deposition to further develop the facts.

3. Ancillary (pendant) Jurisdiction = lawsuits asserting both state and federal claims.

Note: Personal jurisdiction in federal civil cases extends throughout the geographical boundaries of the United States. Further, under certain limited circumstances, federal personal jurisdiction can extend to defendants who reside outside the United States. This issue can become extremely complicated, as sometimes treaties and other international agreements must be considered.

The Erie Doctrine

When a lawsuit is brought in federal court based upon diversity of citizenship, the federal court is to apply federal procedural law and the appropriate state substantive law. This rule is known as The Erie Doctrine.

Therefore assume that there is a motor vehicle accident in Houston, Texas involving a resident of Texas and a resident of Florida. If a lawsuit is brought in federal court, then the federal court shall apply federal procedural law (Federal Rules of Civil Procedure and Federal Rules of Evidence) and the substantive law (in this case, personal injury law) of Texas.

Removal

Exclusive Jurisdiction means that only one court has jurisdiction over a case. Concurrent Jurisdiction means that qamore than one court has jurisdiction over a case.

Sometimes a case may be brought in either federal court or state court because there is concurrent jurisdiction. If the plaintiff files the suit in state court, the defendant may elect to defend the case in the state court or force the transfer of the case to federal court. The election by a defendant to force the transfer of a case from state court to a federal court is called removal.

Step Five: Determine the Correct Venue

Venue refers to the physical location of the court where a case will be heard. For example, there are 254 counties in Texas and each county has a District Court. Therefore, in Texas, venue refers to the specific county where the suit is filed. Federal trial courts are organized by districts, so federal venue has to do with the district where the suit is filed.

Texas has strict venue rules which may be found in the Texas Civil Practice and Remedies Code and the Texas Rules of Civil Procedure.

Federal venue rules are more flexible and are based upon the most convenient forum, meaning the location where the parties reside, where the incident occurred, where the majority of witnesses or other evidence is located, or some combination of these factors. The federal judge has significant discretion to decide the most convenient forum.

Step Six: Determine the Correct Identities of the Parties to the Suit

It is very important for a party bringing a lawsuit to correctly identify the party being sued. Sometimes it is easy to identify the correct defendant and other times it is not. For example, assume the plaintiff was injured in a fall at an Exxon gas station/convenience store. Who is the correct defendant? Exxon? But…which Exxon corporate entity? Exxon, Inc.? Exxon, USA, Inc.? Normally, each corporation is a separate legal person and the correct corporation must be named. Let's throw another "monkey wrench" into the equation. Are the premises where the plaintiff fell operated by an Exxon entity or is it a franchise operated by a completely different business entity? If the correct defendant is not sued by the deadline imposed by the statute of limitations, then the plaintiff is prevented from asserting the suit.

Step Seven: Determine the Correct Capacities of the Parties to the Suit

Depending upon the circumstances, a party may sue or be sued in one or more different capacities. Consider the name (style) of the following lawsuit:

Mary Jones, Individually, as Executor of the Estate of John Jones, Deceased, and As Next Friend to Billy Jones, A Minor
VS.
ABC Corporation

In the style of the case referenced above, there is only one plaintiff – Mary Jones. However, Mary Jones is suing in three separate and distinct capacities.

It is important before filing suit to determine the correct capacities of the parties to the suit. Some common capacities in which a person may sue or be sued are:

- individual capacity;
- d/b/a = doing business as (the assumed name of a business);
- executor = a person appointed to a will to process the estate of a deceased person
- administrator = a person appointed by a court to administer the estate of a deceased person where there is not a valid will'
- trustee = this term has various meanings, depending upon the circumstances of the case;
- as next friend = one who brings a suit on behalf of a child;
- guardian = one who is appointed by a court to manage the personal and/or financial welfare of another.

THE TEXAS STATE COURTS

Each state in the United States is empowered to create its own court systems, consistent with the United States Constitution. Therefore, state court systems differ from each other, not only in structure and procedure, but also in the names given to specific courts.

Despite the differences, all court systems in the United States have certain commonalities. First, each court system has trial courts and appeals courts. A trial court is the court that first decides a case. An appeals court reviews cases appealed from lower courts to determine if there has been an error.

Secondly, each court system has its own written rules of procedure and evidence.

Finally, the courts in each court system issue judgments. A **verdict** is the factual findings in a particular case, which is usually made by a jury. However, a verdict does not decide a case. Rather, a **judgment**, which is a legal decision made by a judge, decides a case. This means that in most instances, a jury verdict is subject to review by the trial judge. Under some circumstances, the judge can overturn or modify the jury verdict. In either event, the case has not been decided until the judge issues a judgment (or in some instances, a dismissal).

Texas has a number of different trial and appeals courts. The discussion of these courts is not intended to provide jurisdictional details (which can be confusing and highly technical in some instances), but rather to identify the general subject matter within the jurisdiction of the courts.

The Texas state **trial courts** are as follows:
1. **District Court** – criminal jurisdiction over felonies. Civil jurisdiction is over divorce cases, cases involving title to land, contested elections, worker's compensation and cases involving amounts in controversy of $200 or more. There are over 450 district courts in Texas.
2. **Constitutional County Court** – these courts can have misdemeanor and juvenile criminal jurisdiction under certain circumstances and have civil jurisdiction over probate and civil cases with $200 to $10,000 in controversy. For technical

reasons, as a matter of government policy, the tendency is to limit the jurisdiction of this court wherever possible in favor of other trial courts. It is required that there be a constitutional county court in each county, so there are 254 of them in Texas.

3. **County Court at Law** – jurisdiction is determined by the legislature and can vary from county to county. Normally, this court has criminal jurisdiction over Class A and B misdemeanors. Its civil jurisdiction can vary, but can include lawsuits in which the amount in dispute is from $200 to $200,000. There is a County Court at Law in many, but not all counties.

4. **Justice Court (Justice of the Peace)** – criminal jurisdiction over Class C misdemeanors. Civil jurisdiction includes eviction suits and small claims from $200 to $10,000. This court can also serve as a magistrate, advising an accused of criminal charges and setting bail, and can sometimes serve as a coroner. There is at least one Justice of the Peace in each county and many counties have four or more such courts.

5. **Municipal Court** – criminal jurisdiction over Class C misdemeanors and virtually no civil jurisdiction. A municipal judge also can serve as a magistrate.

6. **Statutory Probate Courts** – these courts are very few in number and exist in populated counties. Jurisdiction is over probate matters. In populated counties, the trial courts sometimes have specialized jurisdiction. In Harris County (Houston), for example, there are District Courts that hear only family law matters and District Courts that only hear criminal matters. The same specialization can exist with respect to the County Courts at Law.

The Texas state **appeal courts** are as follows:

1. **Court of Appeals** – this first stage appeals court has had criminal jurisdiction over all criminal appeals, except death penalty cases, since 1981. It also has jurisdiction over civil appeals. There are fourteen such courts located in cities throughout Texas.

2. **Court of Criminal Appeals** – located in Austin, this is the highest level Texas state criminal appeals court. Jurisdiction is limited to criminal cases.

3. **Supreme Court of Texas** – located in Austin, this court has civil

appeals jurisdiction over questions of law. This court also
serves as the licensing authority for Texas attorneys.

In an odd way, the County Court at Law and the Constitutional County Court
sometimes act as appeal courts. Because the Justice Court and Municipal Court
normally do not have court reporters to make a verbatim record of the proceedings,
appeals from their decisions can be made to the county courts. Because there is no
record that can be reviewed on appeal, the party making the appeal receives a new trial
in the county courts, as if there had never been a trial in the Justice or Municipal Court.
This "appeal", which creates the right to a new trial in a court of record, is called
trial de novo.

REMEDIES

The purpose of a lawsuit is to seek some form of "relief" from the court. The types of relief that can be granted by a court are called **remedies**.

The most common remedy sought in a civil lawsuit is **damages**. Simply stated, "damages" means money. Most of the time, when a person sues for damages, he/she is seeking **compensatory damages**, which means compensation for a loss of some sort. When a person seeks recovery of medical expenses in a personal injury case, he/she is seeking compensatory damages. There are other types of damages. **Statutory damages** refer to damages authorized by a specific statute. **Punitive damages**, also called **exemplary damages**, may be awarded under certain circumstances, not to compensate, but to punish a party for serious misconduct.

There are other specific terms used in describing types of damages. The term **liquidated damages** (or "economic" damages) refers to damages that can be calculated to a sum certain, such as the amount due on a credit card account. The term **unliquidated damages** (or non-economic damages) means damages that cannot easily be calculated to a certain sum, such as damages for mental anguish.

While the most common remedy sought in a civil lawsuit is damages, the court can grant many other types of relief. The court can grant recovery of **attorney's fees** when such a recovery is agreed to by parties to a contract or authorized by statute.

Another common remedy sought in a civil lawsuit is **injunctive relief**. An **injunction** is a court order, the violation of which can result in fine or imprisonment. Most injunctions are **prohibitory**, which means the court orders a person not to commit certain conduct. In some instances the court can issue an injunction that is **mandatory**, which means the court orders a person to take specific action.

Injunctions can be issued in stages. A **temporary restraining order (TRO)** is an emergency injunction that can be issued without a hearing. A TRO is only good for a short period of time, normally until a hearing can be scheduled. A **temporary injunction** requires a hearing and, if it is granted, can be in effect as long as the lawsuit is pending. The purpose of a temporary injunction is to preserve the status quo while

the lawsuit is pending. **A permanent injunction** means just what it says and requires a trial before it can be issued.

It should be noted that juries do not determine whether or not an injunction should be issued. Injunctive relief is determined by the court alone. Injunctive relief comes from **equity jurisprudence**, which means law that was influenced by the early Christian Church, and the church's legal processes did not include juries.

Receivership is a remedy in which the court orders that control of a business or financial estate be placed under the control of a person designated by the court.

Garnishment is a remedy in which a third person holding funds for someone is ordered to disburse those funds to such parties as are ordered by the court.

Partition is a remedy whereby the court orders a division of property (usually real estate) amongst co-owners,

Recission is a remedy whereby the court orders cancellation of some agreement or obligation.

Restitution is a remedy often granted along with recission, orders the parties back into the financial position they were in before the obligation was rescinded.

Specific Performance is a remedy in which the court compels a party to fulfill a contractual obligation. This remedy is usually limited to contracts for the sale of real estate.

Declaratory Judgment is a remedy whereby the court decides the obligations of parties in advance of an actual violation by one of the parties. For example, an insurance company, rather than deny coverage of a claim, can seek a declaratory judgment as to whether the claim is covered by the policy of insurance. This permits the insurance company to act on the claim without breaching the insurance contract. Declaratory relief is only permitted in limited situations because a court normally does give advisory opinions. Courts normally decides only actual, not potential, disputes.

There are many other remedies that can be granted by courts, depending upon the type and circumstances of a case.

ACTIONS AND PARTIES

Once suit is filed, a variety of other actions can be filed, not as separate suits, but within the same suit. This practice of consolidating all claims between parties into a single suit is normally required by the courts in order to avoid multiple trials between the same parties and/or multiple trials arising out of the same incident. The various actions that may be brought within the same lawsuit are as follows:

Counterclaim – where a Defendant sues a Plaintiff in the same suit. If a counterclaim is filed, the Plaintiff is also a **Counter-Defendant** and the Defendant is also a **Counter-Plaintiff**.

Cross-Action (or **Cross-Claim**) – where a Defendant sues another Defendant in the same suit. If a cross action if filed, the Defendant who files the cross action is also a **Cross-Plaintiff** and the Defendant who is sued in a cross action is also a **Cross-Defendant**.

Joinder – refers to bringing someone into an existing suit. For example, if a Plaintiff sues another party after filing the initial lawsuit, a new Defendant is brought into the suit. This is one type of joinder. When a Plaintiff brings a new Defendant into the suit, there is no special party designation – the new party is a Defendant. However, when a Defendant brings a new party to a suit, it is called a third-party action.

Third Party Action – where a Defendant sues someone who was not previously in the lawsuit. A Defendant who files a third party action is also a **Third Party Plaintiff**.

Intervention – where a person enters a lawsuit seeking a derivative right of a person who is already a party to the lawsuit. For example, a spouse of a person who filed a personal injury lawsuit could file an intervention seeking a community property interest in any recovery. A person who files an intervention is called an **Intervenor**.

Interpleader – imagine that a person died and the deceased left a life insurance policy of $100,000. However, a dispute arose because several people claimed to be the sole beneficiary under the insurance policy. When a party holding funds is subject to competing claims to the funds, the party holding the funds can deposit the proceeds with the court so that the court can determine who is entitled to the funds. This type of action is called an **Interpleader**. The party who files the interpleader is called a **Stakeholder**.

It is critical for someone dealing with civil litigation to know the types of actions that can be filed within a lawsuit and the various designations of party status. Why? Because the terminology of actions and parties is constantly used in litigation. The terms are routinely found in the rules of procedure, legal documents and in memos by attorneys to paralegals. One cannot function in the litigation environment without the ability to instantly recognize these terms and their meaning.

PLEADINGS

Introduction

A pleading is a document that requests some form of relief that is filed with a court. Pleadings include amended pleadings, supplemental pleadings and responses to pleadings.

Common Types of Pleadings

The following are common types of pleadings used in civil lawsuits throughout the United Sates.

1. Plaintiff's Original Petition (called Complaint in federal court) = this is the pleading that begins the lawsuit.
2. Counterclaim = where a defendant sues a plaintiff in the same suit.
3. Cross-Claim (or Cross-Action) = where a defendant sues a defendant in the same suit.
4. Third Party Action = where a defendant sues someone who was not previously in the lawsuit. Note: when a party is added to a lawsuit, it is called a joinder.
5. Intervention = where someone enters a lawsuit seeking a derivative right of one of the parties to the suit.
6. Interpleader = where someone holding funds subject to completing claims enters a lawsuit and deposits the funds with the court for proper disbursement.
7. The response to any of the above pleadings, called an Answer, is also a pleading.

Parts of a Pleading

1. Caption = located at the top of the first page of a pleading, contains the case number (also called "cause number", the style of the case, and the court designation).
2. Title = each pleading must have a title, located just below the caption.
3. Body = sets forth factual background, cause(s) of action and requested remedies.

Amendment and Supplementation of Pleadings

Pleadings may be amended or supplemented. A supplemental pleading adds to an existing pleading. Example:

- First Supplement to Plaintiff's Original Petition

An amended pleading completely replaces the previous pleading. Example:

- Plaintiff's First Amended Original Petition

A party to a lawsuit may add to a pleading by supplementation or amendment. However, a pleading may be corrected only by an amendment.

In Texas state civil cases, a party does not need to obtain court permission to amend or supplement a pleading, as long as it is done within required deadlines. However, in federal cases, in order to amend or supplement pleadings, a motion must be filed with the court seeking permission to amend or supplement.

Counsel of Record = the attorney who is officially representing a party in a matter before a court. Once an attorney becomes counsel of record, he/she may not withdraw without court approval. In federal court, the counsel of record is referred to as attorney in charge.

Pro Se = refers to a party to a lawsuit who is representing himself/herself without an attorney. Note: except in Justice Court, a corporation may not appear pro se, but instead must appear through an attorney.

SOME GENERAL RULES PERTAINING TO PLEADINGS

Normally, the Plaintiff can go to trial only on those claims set forth in the petition.

Pleadings can be **amended** or **supplemented**. An **amended pleading** takes the place of the previous pleading. For example: if the **Plaintiff's Original Petition** is amended, it becomes the **Plaintiff's First Amended Original Petition**. If supplemented, the supplement is entitled **First Supplement to Plaintiff's Original Petition**. Please note that a supplement cannot change a pleading, only add to it. In order to change a pleading, the pleading must be amended.

In some states, such as Texas, a Defendant can properly challenge a lawsuit by filing an unsworn **general denial** pursuant to Rule 92, Texas Rules of Civil Procedure. However, in some other states and the federal system, the answer must respond specifically to each allegation. Further, in certain situations, the answer to a lawsuit must be verified (sworn to). Examples are answers to suits on sworn accounts and answers to suits which deny the genuineness of one's signature. Other answers requiring verification are set forth in Rule 93, Texas Rules of Civil Procedure.

A Defendant to a lawsuit may, in addition to filing a general denial, assert affirmative defenses. An affirmative defense is a set of facts that limits or eliminates liability. A Defendant cannot assert an affirmative defense at trial unless the Defendant has stated the defense in his/her answer to the suit. The Defendant, not the Plaintiff, has the burden of proving an affirmative defense.

PLAINTIFF'S ORIGINAL PETITION BY THE NUMBERS

The following are references to the Texas Rules of Civil Procedure (TRCP) that pertain to petitions. Please note that in most instances the references paraphrase the rules.

A civil suit in the district or county court shall be commenced by a petition filed in the office of the clerk. **RULE 22, TRCP**

A party can sue or be sued in its assumed name. The true name of the party can be substituted upon motion by a party or sua sponte (referring to when a judge takes action without being requested to do so). **RULE 28, TRCP**

Minors, lunatics, idiots, or persons non compos mentis (referring to persons, such as children, who are not legally competent to bring a lawsuit), who have no legal guardian may sue and be represented by "next friend". **RULE 44, TRCP**

Pleadings which set forth claims for relief, such as petitions, counterclaims, cross actions and third party claims shall contain: (a) a short statement of the cause of action sufficient to give fair notice of claim involved; (b) state the proper range of damages claimed per the rule; (c) a demand for judgment and all other relief to which the party deems himself/herself entitled.
RULE 47, TRCP

Note: In Texas state courts, all Plaintiff's Original Petitions must specify whether discovery is to be conducted under Discovery Control Plan Levels 1, 2, or 3 of **RULE 190.1, TRCP. RULE 190.2, TRCP**

Level 1 Discovery Control Plan applies to cases in which the monetary relief sought is $50,000 or less, not including costs, pre-judgment interest or attorney's fees or a "fast track case" per Rule 169, TRCP. Also applies to divorce suits not involving children in which the marital estate is not more than $50,000. **RULE 190.3, TRCP**

Level 2 Discovery Control Plan applies to cases not subject to the Level 1 Discovery

Level 2 Discovery Control Plan applies to cases not subject to the Level 1 Discovery Plan. **RULE 190.4, TRCP**

Level 3 Discovery Control Plan applies to cases in which the discovery plan has been tailored to the specific case by an order of the trial court.

NO. 2016-10341

GRANT WILLIAMS	§	IN THE DISTRICT COURT
	§	
VS.	§	HARRIS COUNTY, TEXAS
	§	
PAUL RAMSEL, ERIC MITCHELL	§	
CUSTOMTECH,INC., and	§	
SAVETECH, INC.	§	129TH JUDICIAL DISTRICT

<u>PLAINTIFF'S ORIGINAL PETITION</u>

TO THE HONORABLE JUDGE OF SAID COURT:

COMES NOW, GRANT WILLIAMS, hereinafter referred to as Plaintiff, complaining of and against PAUL RAMSEL, ERIC MITCHELL, CUSTOMTECH, INC., and SAVETECH, INC., hereinafter referred to as Defendants, and would respectfully show this Court the following:

I.

Pursuant to Rule 190.1, Texas Rules of Civil Procedure, the Plaintiff's hereby advises that discovery is intended to be conducted under DISCOVERY CONTROL PLAN LEVEL 2, as referenced in Rule 190.3, Texas Rules of Civil Procedure.

II.

Plaintiff, GRANT WILLIAMS, is a resident of Harris County, Texas.

Defendant, PAUL RAMSEL, is a resident of Harris County, Texas and may be served with citation at the following address: 4417 Martin, Houston, Texas 77007.

Defendant, ERIC MITCHELL, is a resident of Harris County, Texas, and may be served with Citation at the following address: 1521 West Gray, Houston, Texas 77019.

Defendant, CUSTOMTECH, INC., is a business duly incorporated under the laws of the State of Texas. Service may be had upon its registered agent, C.T. Corporations Systems, 500 Dallas, Houston, Harris County, Texas 77002.

Defendant, SAVETECH, INC., is a business duly incorporated under the laws of the State of Texas. Service may be had upon its registered agent, U.S. Corporation Systems, 1622 Fannin, Houston, Harris County, Texas 77002.

III.

This Court has jurisdiction over the subject matter of this suit. The amount in controversy is within the jurisdictional limits of this Court. Pursuant to Rule 47(c)(4), TRCP, the Plaintiff seeks monetary relief over $200, 000 but less than $1,000,000.

Venue is proper as the acts or omissions complained of occurred in Harris County, Texas.

IV.

On or about June 20, 2014, the Plaintiff entered into a written contract with Defendants, ERIC MITCHELL, PAUL RAMSEL, and CUSTOMTECH, INC., whereby the parties agreed that the Plaintiff would assist these Defendants in the selling of CUSTOMTECH, INC.

As part of the written contract between the parties, the Plaintiff was to receive fifteen (15) percent of the gross sales price of the company.

On or about February 20, 2015, the Plaintiff introduced the Defendants, ERIC MITCHELL, PAUL RAMSEL, and CUSTOMTECH, INC., to the representatives of Defendant, SAVETECH, INC.

On or about July 18, 2015, without telling the Plaintiff, the Defendants ERIC MITCHELL, PAUL RAMSEL, and CUSTOMTECH, INC., signed an agreement to sell the company to Defendant SAVETECH, INC., for $32.5 million.

8-4

On or About August 5, 2015, through October 4, 2015, the Plaintiff attempted on numerous occasions, without success, to contact the Defendants.

On or about October 20, 2015, the Plaintiff contacted the president of SAVETECH, INC., who informed him of the sale. At this time, the Plaintiff was informed that SAVETECH, INC. disbursed the agreed amount of funds to the Defendants, PAUL RAMSEL and ERIC MITCHELL for the purchase of CUSTOMTECH, INC.

On or about October 28, 2015, the Plaintiff received a letter from the Defendants denying the validity of the written contract. At this time, the Plaintiff was informed that SAVETECH, INC. disbursed the agreed amount of funds to the Defendants, PAUL RAMSEL and ERIC MITCHELL for the purchase of CUSTOMTECH, INC.

V.

The Plaintiff asserts that the Defendants breached the contract by failing to pay the monies to the Plaintiff as promised in the contract.

The Plaintiff further asserts breach of fiduciary duty owed to him by the Defendants with respect to Plaintiff's percentage of the gross proceeds of the sale.

The Plaintiff further alleges fraud on the part of the Defendants in that they intentionally misrepresented that Plaintiff would receive a specific commission when they had no intention of paying the commission. The Plaintiff expended time, talent and efforts in reliance upon said representations.

The Plaintiff further alleges that Defendants, without authority, wrongfully exercised control over the Plaintiff's property, namely the funds from the sale of CUSTOMTECH, INC., that had been assigned to Plaintiff.

The Plaintiff alleges that the Defendants conspired to commit the wrongful conduct alleged and therefore, the Defendants are jointly and severally liable to the Plaintiff.

VI.

Pursuant to Chapter 41 of the Texas Civil Practices and Remedies Code, the Plaintiff seeks exemplary damages from each Defendant in addition to any actual damages, past, present and future.

VII.

The Plaintiff seek pre-judgment and post judgment interest at the maximum legal rate.

VIII.

The Plaintiff hereby demands trial by jury. The Plaintiff tenders herewith a jury fee pursuant to Rule 216, Texas Rules of Civil Procedure.

IX.

The Defendant's actions have made it necessary for the Plaintiff to secure the services of Thomas Williams, a licensed attorney, for the purpose of enforcing the Plaintiff's rights herein. The Defendants should be ordered to pay, and the Plaintiff should have judgment for, Plaintiff's reasonable and necessary attorney's fees.

WHEREFORE, PREMISES CONSIDERED, the Plaintiff prays that the Defendants be cited to appear and answer herein and that upon trial of this cause that the Plaintiff recover his actual, special, general and punitive damages; pre-judgment and post-judgment interest at the maximum legal rate; reasonable attorney's fees; costs of court; and whatever other and further relief, at law or in equity to which the Plaintiff may show himself justly entitled.

Respectfully submitted

POUNDS, DALE AND WILLIAMS

BY: _____
Thomas Williams
State Bar No. 17444800
440 Louisiana, Suite 1400
Houston, Texas 77002
Telephone: (713) 223-2100
Facsimile: (713) 223-2101
E-Mail: tom@pdw.com

ATTORNEYS FOR PLAINTIFF

FILING SUIT, SERVICE OF PROCESS, AND ANSWER DEADLINE

Filing Suit
A Lawsuit is to be filed with the appropriate clerk of the court.
- Texas State District Court: District Clerk
- Texas State County Court: County Clerk
- Texas State Justice Court: Clerk of the Justice Court
- Federal Court: Clerk of the U. S. District Court

E-Filing (Electronic Filing)
All federal filings must be e-filed through the designated e-filing system.

E-filing is mandatory in Texas State civil cases brought in district and county courts and the mandated process should be completed in all of Texas' 254 counties by sometime in 2016.

Normally, when the lawsuit is initially filed, filing fees must be paid to the clerk. The amount of the filing fees can vary, depending upon the court system, and the nature of the suit. Normally, the clerk's website will have information as to the amount of the filing fees.

Please note that in civil cases, if a party to the suit desires a jury trial a jury fee must be paid within a specified period of time. For example, Rule 216, Texas Rules of Civil Procedure, requires that a party to a suit in district or county court who desires a jury trial must: request a jury trial in writing and pay a jury fee at least 30 days before trial. Failure of a party to timely request a jury trial and pay the required jury fee will result in the case being decided by a bench trial, which is a trial by a judge without a jury.

When a lawsuit is filed, the clerk file stamps the lawsuit (which shows the date, and sometimes the time, that the lawsuit was filed) and assigns the lawsuit a case number. In situations where there are multiple courts with the same jurisdiction, the clerk will assign the case to a specific court. Note: anytime a pleading or other document is filed with the clerk, obtain a file-stamped copy of what is filed, in case the document filed is lost. As electronic filing of lawsuits and related documents (e-filing) replaces the filing of hard copies of documents, it is suggested that downloading of hard copies of what is

filed, bearing the date and time filed, should be done for backup verification.

Once a lawsuit is filed with the clerk, it becomes a case on the court's docket, which means the collection of cases pending before a particular court.

Service of Process

The United States Constitution requires that before any person may be deprived of "life, liberty, or property", the person has the right to due process of law. One very important component of due process is fair notice of the complaint against the party being charged in criminal law or sued in civil law. Since a lawsuit is a type of complaint against someone, and often seeks the property of the person being sued, in the form of damages, fair notice of the lawsuit is a constitutional requirement.

In Texas, there are a number of authorized methods of serving a lawsuit. They are as follows:

1. Personal service upon the Defendant by sheriff or constable;
2. Personal service upon the Defendant by a private process server authorized by the court;
3. Service upon the Defendant by certified mail, return receipt requested (or by registered mail), sent by a sheriff or constable;
4. Service in a manner authorized by court order (Rule 106, TRCP); Note: this is commonly referred to as **substituted service** and is usually only permitted after efforts at personal service have been unsuccessful.
5. Service by "publication" in a publication of general circulation. Note: this method of service is normally limited to situations in which the identity of the party to be served is unknown (such as an unknown heir in a probate case) or no other method of service has been successful.

In Texas, when a lawsuit is filed, the clerk prepares a document known (in Texas) as a citation, which is a type of formal legal process that gives the Defendant official notice of the lawsuit. One copy of the citation is attached to the lawsuit and served upon the Defendant. Another copy of the citation is filled out by the person who served the Defendant, verifying the date and time of service, and this copy is filed with the clerk for placement in the court's file.

09/19/2[?]

Answer Deadline

Under most circumstances, when someone is sued in Texas state district or county court, the Defendant must file a written answer to the suit by no later than 10:00 a.m. on the first Monday following twenty (20) days after service. In the event that the Defendant fails to answer on time, the Plaintiff may seek a default judgment.

How does one count the days? Rule 4 of the Texas Rules of Civil Procedure sets forth a universal standard for counting all deadlines. Summarized, the rule operates as follows: in counting the days, the first day (for example, the day something such as a lawsuit or motion is received) does not count. The last day does count, unless the last day falls on a Saturday, Sunday or holiday. If the last day falls on a Saturday, Sunday or holiday, the last day becomes the next business day.

Normally, when a party to a suit files a pleading with the court, the party is said to have made an appearance before the court. Once parties make an appearance before the court, the Texas Rules of Civil Procedure permit the parties to send future pleadings and other documents without the formalities required in serving the original lawsuit. Normally, once parties have made an appearance, service of pleadings and other documents are simply sent back and forth between the attorneys for the parties by some manner that can be verified, such as certified mail, return receipt requested, messenger and overnight mail. Pleadings and documents can be sent by facsimile and e-mail, provided there is some verifiable means used. Often, lawyers will send pleadings or documents by both facsimile and certified mail, return receipt requested, to insure verification.

The Texas Rules of Civil Procedure require that when pleadings and pre-trial discovery documents are sent between the lawyers representing the parties that there be a certificate of service attached to the pleading or document. The certificate of service is certification by the attorney sending the document or pleading as to the date and manner in which it was sent to the other party's attorney. See: Rules 21 and 21a, of the Texas Rules of Civil Procedure.

Numerous examples of certificates of service are contained in later sections of this book.

DEFENDANT'S ANSWER TO PETITION BY THE NUMBERS

In most instances, a Defendant may answer a suit filed in Texas state court by unsworn general denial. If the Plaintiff amends or supplements a petition, the Defendant is not required to further respond by amendment or supplementation.
RULE 92, Texas Rules of Civil Procedure

The Defendant's answer may also include motions, such as special appearance, plea to the jurisdiction, plea in abatement, motion to transfer venue and special exceptions
RULE 85, Texas Rules of Civil Procedure

Sometimes, a Defendant must file a sworn answer to a suit. Such situations include denial of legal capacity, denial of corporate status, denial of a sworn account, allegations of usury (charging illegal rate of interest), denial of an assumed name, etc. Situations in which a Defendant must file a sworn answer are stated in
RULE 93, Texas Rules of Civil Procedure

The filing of a general denial by a Defendant creates the legal obligation on the part of the Plaintiff to prove the allegations in the petition by a preponderance of evidence. However, if the Defendant desires to assert an **affirmative defense** (a set of facts that limit or eliminate liability), the Defendant must specify the defense in his/her answer.
RULE 94, Texas Rules of Civil Procedure

A party to a suit who is subjected to a counterclaim or cross action is not required to answer unless the party intends to assert an affirmative defense or a sworn answer. A party to a suit who does not answer a counterclaim or cross claim is presume to have issued a general denial. **RULE 92, Texas Rules of Civil Procedure**

GRANT WILLIAMS	§	IN THE DISTRICT COURT
	§	
VS.	§	HARRIS COUNTY, TEXAS
	§	
PAUL RAMSEL, ERIC MITCHELL	§	
CUSTOMTECH,INC., and	§	
SAVETECH, INC.	§	129TH JUDICIAL DISTRICT

DEFENDANT, PAUL RAMSEL'S ORIGINAL ANSWER

COMES NOW, PAUL RAMSEL, a Defendant in this cause, and does hereby answer as follows:

I.

Pursuant to Rule 92, Texas Rules of Civil Procedure, this Defendant does hereby enter a general denial and places the Plaintiff upon his proof.

II.

This Defendant does hereby assert the affirmative defense of failure of consideration.

WHEREFORE, PREMISES CONSIDERED, Defendant, Paul Ramsel, prays that the Plain-tiff take nothing by his cause; that this Defendant recover his costs of court; and, this Defendant further prays for general relief.

Respectfully submitted
MARKS & SCHON, L.L.P.

BY: _____
Jennifer Schon
State Bar No. 12238640
4400 Pease, Suite 1100
Houston, Texas 77002
Telephone: (713) 867-5309
Facsimile: (713) 867-5308
E-Mail: schon@mandr.com

ATTORNEYS FOR DEFENDANT,
PAUL RAMSEL

10-2

CERTIFICATE OF SERVICE

I hereby certify that a true and correct copy of the foregoing was sent to opposing

counsel by electronic mail on March 7, 2016.

BY: _____

JENNIFER SCHON

DEFENDANT'S CHALLENGES TO PLAINTIFF'S PETITION

Introduction

Once a lawsuit is filed, it becomes a public record and may only be disposed of in a formal manner, in accordance with law.

There are two basic ways to dispose of (end) a lawsuit.
1. **Judgment** = a legal decision by a judge on the merits of a case;
2. **Dismissal** = disposition of a case without determining its merits.

There are various types of judgments and dismissals, which will be discussed later. Note: a verdict does not dispose of a case. A verdict consists of the factual findings in a case, usually made by a jury. A verdict must be translated into a legal judgment by the judge.

Motions That Attack/Challenge the Plaintiff's Petition

A motion is a request to the court for relief in connection with a pending case. There are numerous types of motions that may be filed during the course of a civil lawsuit.

Certain motions attack/challenge the plaintiff's petition. These motions are as follows:
1. Special Appearance = a motion that challenges the court's personal jurisdiction. In Texas, this motion must be filed either before the filing of the answer, or at the same time as the filing of the answer. If any pleading is filed before the special appearance, then the defendant has consented to the court's personal jurisdiction and the special appearance will be denied.

    Note: Special appearances are rare in federal cases because the scope of the federal court's personal jurisdiction extends throughout the United States.

2. Plea To The Jurisdiction = motion that challenges the court's subject matter jurisdiction. This motion should be filed as soon as the defendant becomes aware that the court does not have jurisdiction.

Note: The federal version of this motion is called motion for involuntary dismissal.

3.   Plea In Abatement = a motion that freezes action in a case. This motion can occur because a bankruptcy was filed by one of the parties to the suit; or, because the parties agreed to submit their dispute to a private party (arbitrator) for resolution; or, because the plaintiff failed to comply with some mandatory requirement before filing suit.

Note: The federal version of this motion is motion to abate.

4.   Motion For Summary Judgment (MSJ) = This is a motion for judgment without trial. There is no presumption of innocence in the civil law so if a party can show that there is no material (significant) fact in dispute, then there is nothing for a jury to decide. In cases where there is no disputed material fact, the judge can decide the case without trial by summary judgment.

Any party can file a MSJ. This is very dangerous motion, which requires strict attention to deadlines. All states and the federal system permit the MSJ in civil cases.

Texas has two distinctive types of MSJs:
a. Standard (Traditional) MSJ – this type of MSJ exists throughout the United States. The party asserting the MSJ must attach evidence to the motion showing that there is no material fact in dispute such that the moving party is entitled to judgment without a trial. Normally, the MSJ must be on file for at least 21 days before it may be ruled upon and the opposing party must file a response at least 7 days before the date of hearing or ruling, or else the MSJ will be granted. The MSJ will be denied if the opposing party timely files a response with evidence showing that there are material facts in dispute such that a trial is required.

Note: The federal version of this motion is motion for summary judgment.

b. No Evidence MSJ – this MSJ is not common outside of Texas. This MSJ may only be filed by a defendant and no evidence may be attached. This type of MSJ asserts that the plaintiff cannot produce any evidence so as to prove one is or more specific elements of the cause of action asserted in the plaintiff's petition. This MSJ is designed to force the plaintiff to make a showing of some evidence of the challenged element so that the defendant will not have to bear the expense of defending a case that cannot be proven at trial. Like the standard MSJ, the No Evidence MSJ must be on file at least 21 days before any hearing or ruling and the plaintiff must respond with appropriate evidence at least 7 days before the motion is to be heard or ruled upon.

Note: The federal version of this motion is motion for involuntary dismissal.

5.   Motion To Transfer Venue = a motion to change the physical location where the suit will be tried. There are strict venue rules that apply to cases filed in Texas state courts, and the court will transfer venue from one county to another if the venue rules so require.

Note: Federal courts have significant discretion regarding the transfer of venue. Normally, the federal courts want cases tried in the most convenient forum, meaning where the most witnesses, parties and evidence are located. Sometimes, a federal motion to transfer venue will be referred to as a motion forum non conveniens.

6.   Special Exceptions = a motion to compel a plaintiff to amend the petition because
    • the petition fails to state a legal claim; or
    • the petition is so vague that it fails to give proper notice

If the court grants the special exceptions, the plaintiff is given a limited time to amend the petition. Should the plaintiff fail to amend the petition as ordered by the court, the court will strike the excepted portion of the petition. If, after the court strikes the excepted portion of the petition, the petition states no cause of action, then the court will dismiss the suit.

Note: In federal court, special exceptions based upon failure to state a legal claim is called a motion for involuntary dismissal and special exceptions based upon vagueness is called motion for more definite statement.

7.   Motion To Dismiss Pursuant to Rule 91a, TRCP = asserts that a cause of action should be dismissed because it has no basis in law or fact.

"A cause of action has no basis in law if the allegations, taken as true, together with inferences reasonably drawn from them do not entitle the claimant to the relief sought. A cause of action has no basis in fact of no reasonable person could believe the facts pleaded." **RULE 91A1, TRCP**

A Motion To Dismiss must be filed within 60 days after the first pleading containing the challenged cause of action is served on the movant; filed at least 21 days before the motion is heard; and granted or denied within 45 days after the motion is filed. **RULE 91A3, TRCP**

If a Motion To Dismiss is heard, the court must grant attorney's fees and costs to the winning party. **RULE 91A7, TRCP**

PRE-TRIAL DISCOVERY – INTRODUCTION

Pre-Trial Discovery is the name of a process whereby parties to a lawsuit obtain information for the purpose of developing and preparing the case for trial. In civil cases filed in Texas state courts, pre-trial discovery is governed primarily by the **Texas Rule of Civil Procedure**, which is a compilation of rules issued by the Supreme Court of Texas.

While pre-trial discovery permits parties to a lawsuit to develop and prepare cases for trial, there are other important reasons for the process. Pre-trial discovery can simplify the issues in a case because it permits the parties to determine which issues in the case are disputed and which issues are not disputed. The purpose of trial is to resolve disputes and pre-trial discovery can limit the number of issues to be tried. For example, consider a personal injury case that arose out of a vehicle accident. Through pre-trial discovery, the names of the owners of the vehicles, the drivers of the vehicles, the date, time and location of the accident, as well as the conditions of the road and weather can be established as undisputed and requiring no proof at trial. This allows the parties to focus on the disputed facts and shortens the length of trial. Often, the more complicated the case, the more beneficial pre-trial discovery is in shortening the trial.

Another purpose of the pre-trial discovery is to promote settlement of disputes, thereby eliminating the need for a trial. Since pre-trial discovery rules permit "discovery" of information pertinent to the case, the parties are more informed as to the likely result if the case does go to trial. Most people do not want to go through a trial if a reasonable settlement based upon the facts and the law can be obtained. Pre-trial discovery allows parties to determine the facts relevant to a case before trial.

Pre-trial discovery as a formal process began in the 1930's in the federal court system and thereafter the state court systems followed suit. Since the 1940's, pre-trial discovery rules applicable to Texas civil cases have expanded and changed to the point that today, pre-trial discovery is a complex process. Lawyers and paralegals working in civil litigation today require specialized training in the pre-trial discovery process. Under ideal circumstances, a case should be won or lost on its substantive merits, not on technical procedural matters. However, times have changed. Mistakes made in pre-trial discovery can affect the outcome of a case.

The most formidable aspect of pre-trial discovery is **meeting deadlines**. Most pre-trial discovery matters are time sensitive. In Texas, as well as in other jurisdictions, the unexcused failure to meet a discovery deadline can result in an **automatic sanction**. These automatic sanctions can include loss of the right to call witnesses at trial and loss of the right to assert or deny certain facts at trial. Stated simply, a case that might otherwise have been won can be lost because a deadline was missed. The failure to meet deadlines not only can cause injury to the client's interests, but can also result in civil liability and ethical disciplinary action upon the attorney guilty of such mistakes. Keep in mind that the consequences of a paralegal's failure to meet a discovery deadline is imputed to the attorney.

It may seem strange that meeting procedural deadlines presents such a formidable chal-lenge in civil trial practice. The reason meeting deadlines is such a problem has to do with volume. The economics of civil trial practice dictate that lawyers have many cases at one time. It is difficult to determine at what point a lawyer has too much to handle. At any rate, most civil trial lawyers have constant deadlines to meet because of the volume of cases most of them have at any one time. Being "busy" is not a defense to missing a deadline. Given the civil trial lawyer's day-to-day deadlines, the role of the paralegal is of critical importance. In the twenty-first century, lawyers and paralegals work as a team in litigation matters.

TYPES OF PRE-TRIAL DISCOVERY

In General

Generally, the types of pre-trial discovery that may be used in the development of civil suits in the United States are similar. This is because pre-trial discovery originated in the federal court system and most states adopted much of the pre-trial discovery practice and termi-nology. There are three major categories of pre-trial discovery:

1. Discovery Requests – these are written requests for information that one party may send to another;
2. Depositions – this refers to testimony under oath taken before trial; and
3. "Other" – this includes matters such as inspections of land and medical examinations of claimants in personal injury cases.

Note: Electronic discovery or e-discovery will be discussed in the last section of the book – "Innovations".

Discovery Requests

There are three types of discovery requests used throughout the United States:
1. Requests For Admission – written requests that a party admit certain facts so that they need not be proven at trial;
2. Interrogatories – refer to written questions or inquiries to a party that are to be answered under oath; and
3. Requests for Production and Inspection – written requests that a party produce speci-fied documents and items for inspection and copying. Most of the time, the items re-quested and produced are documents. However, now that we are in the digi-tal/elec tronic age, production requests also include e-mails, text mails and other writings and depictions in digital form.

Texas Pre-trial Discovery

Rule 192.1 of the Texas Rules of Civil Procedure describes the forms of pre-trial dis-covery as follows:
(a) requests for disclosure;
(b) requests for production and inspection;

(c)   requests and motions for entry upon and examination of real property;

(d)   interrogatories;

(e)   requests for admission;

(f)   oral or written depositions; and

(g)   motions for mental or physical examinations.

AGREEMENTS BETWEEN COUNSEL

Most trial lawyers are counsel of record in numerous suits at any given time and each suit impos-es numerous deadlines. How do trial lawyers juggle so many "balls" day after day? One answer is by having a well-trained paralegal. Often, it is the paralegal who monitors deadlines and en-sures that the trial lawyer is aware of them well in advance. Another answer is found in Rule 11, Texas Rules of Civil Procedure, which is as follows: **Rule 11. Agreements to Be In Writing**

"Unless otherwise provided in these rules, no agreement between attorneys or parties touch-ing any suit pending will be enforced unless it be in writing, signed and filed with the papers as part of the record, or unless it be made in open court and entered of record."

This very brief rule of procedure has major implications. First, it recognizes that there will be agreements between attorneys and parties with respect to pending l awsuits. In Texas state practice, these agreements are commonly called Rule 11 Agreements. The most common use of such agreements is to extend the response deadlines with respect to pre-trial discovery requests. The second major implication of Rule 11 is that agreements will not be enforced unless the re-quirements of the rule are met. For the trial lawyer and paralegal, this means that you must obtain a signed agreement in writing **before** any deadline expires or else you are at the mercy of the op-posing counsel.

There is no required format for a Rule 11 agreement. It may be done by letter (and this is often the case) or in a pleading format, complete with caption, title and so forth. Examples of both formats are contained in the pages that follow.

Please note: Rule 11 agreements normally cannot be used to change a trial date without the approval of the trial judge.

In some jurisdictions, agreements between counsel are called **stipulations**.

No. 2015-11275

MARY SMITH	§	IN THE DISTRICT COURT OF
	§	
VS.	§	HARRIS COUNTY, TEXAS
	§	
JOHN DOE	§	190TH JUDICIAL DISTRICT

RULE 11 AGREEMENT

The Plaintiff and Defendant, by and through their counsel of record hereby make the following agreements pursuant to Rule 11, TRCP.

1. The deadline for Plaintiff, Mary Smith, to answer interrogatories is extended, without waiver of objections or privileges, to July 25, 2016; and

2. The deadline for Defendant, John Doe, to answer interrogatories is extended, without waiver of objections or privileges, to July 29, 2016.

THOMAS B. SWANSON
State Bar No. 19555900
1302 Waugh Drive, PMB 383
Houston, Texas 77019
Telephone: (713) 447-7926
Facsimile: (855) 422-4466
E-Mail: velva53@hotmail.com

ANNE JONES
State Bar No. 14663725
2701 Fannin
Houston, Texas 77002
Telephone: (713) 224-2000
Facsimile: (713) 224-2101
E-Mail: attyajones@gmail.com

ATTORNEY FOR PLAINTIFF

ATTORNEY FOR DEFENDANT

SAMPLE AGREEMENT BETWEEN COUNSEL

REQUESTS FOR ADMISSIONS

The purpose of **Requests for Admission** is to eliminate the need to spend time proving un-disputed matters.

Rule 198.2, Texas Rules of Civil Procedure, provides that responses to **Requests for Admissions** must be made within thirty (30) days after receipt.

Rule 192.1, Texas Rules of Civil Procedure, provides that a request can include any man-ner within the scope of discovery, including statements of fact, opinions, the application of law to fact and genuineness of documents.

> There are five possible responses to a request for admissions:
> 1. admit;
> 2. deny;
> 3. objection;
> 4. assertion of privilege;
> 5. inability to admit or deny for some specified reasons; or
> 6. some combination of the above.

Claiming an inability to admit or deny a request due to lack of information is not proper unless the responding party states that "a reasonable inquiry was made but that information known or easily obtainable is insufficient to enable the responding party to admit or deny". **Rule 198.2(b), Texas Rules of Civil Procedure.**

Rule 198.2(2), Texas Rules of Civil Procedure, is so important that it is quoted below in its entirety:

"**Effect of failure to respond.** If a response is not timely served, the request is considered admitted without necessity of a court order,"

While **Rule 198.3, Texas Rules of Civil Procedure**, gives the court authority to permit withdrawal or amendment of an admission. However, in practice, the courts are reluctant to grant such relief. This means that special attention must be paid to this form of discovery to avoid missing the deadline for responding.

NO. 2016-10341

GRANT WILLIAMS	§	IN THE DISTRICT COURT OF
	§	
VS.	§	HARRIS COUNTY, TEXAS
	§	
PAUL RAMSEL, ET AL	§	129TH JUDICIAL DISTRICT

REQUESTS FOR ADMISSIONS TO PLAINTIFF

TO: Grant Williams, Plaintiff, by and through his attorney of record, Thomas Williams, Pounds, Dale and Williams, 440 Louisiana, Suite 1400, Houston, Texas 77002.

Pursuant to Rule 198, Texas Rules of Civil Procedure, the attached requests for admissions are hereby propounded upon you. Said requests must be responded to separately within thirty (30) days or else said requests are admitted without the necessity of a court order.

You are reminded that these requests for admissions are continuing, pursuant to Rule 193.5, Texas Rules of Civil Procedure.

Respectfully submitted,

MARKS & SCHON, L.L.P.

_____
BY: Jennifer Schon
State Bar No. 1238640
4400 Pease, Suite 1100
Houston, Texas 77002
Telephone: (713) 867-5309
Facsimile: (713) 867-5308
E-Mail: schon@markschon.com

ATTORNEYS FOR DEFENDANT

15-2

IT IS REQUESTED THAT YOU ADMIT THE FOLLOWING:

1.   That you did not complete the sale of Customtech, Inc. to Savetech, Inc.

RESPONSE:

2.   That you did not complete the sale of Customtech, Inc. to anyone.

RESPONSE:

3.   It was agreed that you would receive no payment of any kind from Customtech, Inc. relating to the sale of Customtech, Inc. unless you completed the sale.

RESPONSE:

CERTIFICATE OF SERVICE

I hereby certify that a true copy of the foregoing was sent to opposing counsel by

messenger on July 28, 2016.

_____

JENNIFER SCHON

15-4

REQUESTS FOR DISCLOSURE

Effective January 1, 1999, a new form of discovery was authorized by the Texas Rules of Civil Procedure. Requests for Disclosure, set forth in Rule 194, Texas Rules of Civil Procedure, permit discovery of the following specific information:

1. The name, address and telephone number of each person having knowledge of relevant facts, along with a brief statement of each identified person's connection with the case;

2. The name, address and telephone number of expert witnesses who are expected to testify, along with a general substance of the expert's mental impressions and opinions (and the basis for the impressions andopinions) and those materials reviewed by and prepared by the expert);

3. The names and addresses of parties and potential parties;

4. Settlement, indemnity and insuring agreements not subject to legal privilege;

5. Witness statements not subject to legal privilege; and

6. Medical bills and records in personal injury cases. Further, in cases where the injured party has provided a defendant with a medical authorization to obtain medical bills and records obtained using the authorization.

Note: The specific language of the information that a party can compel to be disclosed is detailed in Rule 194.2(a) through (l), Texas Rules of Civil Procedure.

Responses to Requests for Disclosure must be made within thirty (30) days, unless the number of documents is unusually large, in which case the responding party must state a reasonable time and place for the production of the documents.

No objection is permitted to a request for disclosure. Rule 194.5, Texas Rules of Civil Procedure.

Requests for Disclosure and responses to same are not to be filed with the court. Rule 191.4, Texas Rules of Civil Procedure.

NO. 2016-10341

GRANT WILLIAMS	§	IN THE DISTRICT COURT OF
	§	
VS.	§	HARRIS COUNTY, TEXAS
	§	
PAUL RAMSEL, ET AL	§	129TH JUDICIAL DISTRICT

DEFENDANT, PAUL RAMSEL'S REQUESTS FOR DISCLOSURE TO PLAINTIFF

TO: Grant Williams, Plaintiff, by and through his attorney of record, Thomas Williams, Pounds, Dale and Williams, 440 Louisiana, Suite 1400, Houston, Texas 77002.

You are hereby requested to provide the information and produce the documents responsive to Rule 194.2(a) through (l), Texas Rules of Civil Procedure within thirty (30) days from receipt of this request.

You are reminded that these requests for disclosure are continuing and that, pursuant to Rule 193.5, Texas Rules of Civil Procedure, that you must amend and/or supplement your answers in the event that you later learn a response is incorrect or if additional responsive information is discovered.

Respectfully submitted,

MARKS & SCHON, L.L.P.

_____
BY: Jennifer Schon
State Bar No. 1238640
4400 Pease, Suite 1100
Houston, Texas 77002
Telephone: (713) 867-5309
Facsimile: (713) 867-5308
E-Mail: schon@markschon.com

ATTORNEYS FOR DEFENDANT

16-2

CERTIFICATE OF SERVICE

I hereby certify that a true copy of the foregoing was sent to opposing counsel by messenger on July 28, 2016.

_____

JENNIFER SCHON

INTERROGATORIES

Interrogatories are written questions to another party to a suit which must be answered by the responding party under oath. In situations in which some of the answers contain information obtained from other persons, the answering party may qualify the oath to reflect that he/she does not have personal knowledge of the information. **Rule 197, Texas Rules of Civil Procedure.**

The number of interrogatories, including subparts, that may be filed upon one party by another party are limited. **Rule 190, Texas Rules of Civil Procedure.**

Answers to interrogatories must be served on the opposing party no later than **thirty** (30) days from receipt. The failure to timely respond can result in loss of the right to object, the right to introduce untimely evidence at trial and court ordered sanctions. **Rules 193.2, 193.6, 197.2, 215, Texas Rules of Civil Procedure,**

Interrogatories and **answers to interrogatories** are not to be filed with the court. **Rule 191.4, Texas Rules of Civil Procedure.**

The party answering interrogatories must make complete responses and must promptly amend or supplement answers if the party later obtains additional responsive information or learns that information previously given was incorrect. **Rules 193.1 and Rule 193.5, Texas Rules of Civil Procedure.**

Answers to Interrogatories may be used only against the party who answered them – for example in summary judgment motions or at trial. **Rule 197.3, Texas Rules of Civil Procedure.**

Note:
1. Normally, answers to interrogatories will consist of information from the client and information obtained by the attorney during the course of investigation and discovery. Since the client must swear to answers to which he/she has knowledge, carefully review the answers with the client to ensure correctness.

2. In almost every case, discovery responses, including supplements and amendments **must** be served upon the opposing party at least thirty (30) days before trial. Therefore, you **must** pay careful attention to this deadline.

NO. 2016-10341

GRANT WILLIAMS	§	IN THE DISTRICT COURT OF
	§	
VS.	§	HARRIS COUNTY, TEXAS
	§	
PAUL RAMSEL, ET AL	§	129TH JUDICIAL DISTRICT

DEFENDANT, PAUL RAMSEL'S INTERROGATORIES TO PLAINTIFF

TO: Grant Williams, Plaintiff, by and through his attorney of record, Thomas Williams, Pounds, Dale and Williams, 440 Louisiana, Suite 1400, Houston, Texas 77002.

Pursuant to Rule 197, Texas Rules of Civil Procedure, the attached interrogatories are hereby propounded upon you to be answered separately, under oath, and said answers to be served upon the underground attorney no later than thirty (30) days from receipt.

You are reminded that the attached interrogatories are continuing and that, pursuant to Rule 193.5, Texas Rules of Procedure, that you must amend and/or supplement your answers in the event that you later learn an answer is incorrect or if additional responsive information is discovered.

Respectfully submitted,

MARKS & SCHON, L.L.P.

_____
BY: Jennifer Schon
State Bar No. 1238640
4400 Pease, Suite 1100
Houston, Texas 77002
Telephone: (713) 867-5309
Facsimile: (713) 867-5308
E-Mail: schon@markschon.com

ATTORNEYS FOR DEFENDANT

17-2

INTERROGATORIES

1.   If you have filed a civil suit against anyone in the last ten years, please state:
   a.   the names of the parties to each such suit;
   b.   the case number of each such suit;
   c.   the specific court in which each such suit was filed;
   d.   a summary of the subject matter of each suit; and
   e.   the ultimate disposition of each suit.

ANSWER:

2.   If anyone has ever filed a civil suit against you in the last ten years, please state:
   a.   the name of the parties to each suit;
   b.   the case number of each such suit;
   c.   the specific court in which each such suit was filed;
   d.   a summary of the subject matter of each suit; and
   e.   the ultimate disposition of each suit.

ANSWER:

3.   If you have been convicted of a felony or misdemeanor involving moral turpitude during the last ten years, please state:
   a.   the name of the parties to each suit;
   b.   the case number of each such suit;
   c.   the specific court in which each such suit was filed;
   d.   a summary of the subject matter of each suit; and
   e.   the ultimate disposition of each suit.

ANSWER:

4.   Please state your full name, date of birth and social security account number.

ANSWER:

_____
                        GRANT WILLIAMS

STATE OF TEXAS

COUNTY OF HARRIS

     BEFORE ME, the undersigned authority, on this day personally appeared, GRANT WILLIAMS; who, after being duly sworn, start upon oath that the answers to the foregoing interrogatories are true and correct.

_____
NOTARY PUBLIC
STATE OF TEXAS

_____
Printed Name of Notary

My Commission Expires:

_____

CERTIFICATE OF SERVICE

I hereby certify that a true copy of the foregoing was sent to opposing counsel by messenger on July 28, 2016.

_____
JENNIFER SCHON

REQUESTS FOR PRODUCTION AND INSPECTION

Requests for Production and Inspection are governed by **Rule 196, Texas Rules of Civil Procedure**. The purposes of this form of discovery are to permit access to tangible items, such as documents, photographs and tape recordings, and access to land.

Requests for Production invoke a two-part compliance process. First, there must be timely written responses to the requests, normally within thirty (30) days from receipt. **Rule 196.2(a), Texas Rules of Civil Procedure**. Secondly, there must be actual production of the items (or copies) requested. The time and place of production must be reasonable and the time and place designated by the requesting party is presumed to be reasonable unless a timely objection is made or the parties involved make a specific written agreement as to the time and place of production. **Rule 196.3, Texas Rules of Civil Procedure**. Again, the normal time period given for production is thirty (30) days.

Rule 196 also permits **entry onto land, inspection** and **photographing, videotaping** and testing, where appropriate for development of a lawsuit. If the parties cannot agree to the time, scope or manner of such matters, a motion can be filed and the court will issue appropriate orders. **Rule 196.7, Texas Rules of Civil Procedure**.

Requests for Production and Inspection, responses to same and items produced are not to be filed with the court. **Rule 191.4, Texas Rules of Civil Procedure**.

NO. 2016-10341

GRANT WILLIAMS	§	IN THE DISTRICT COURT OF
	§	
VS.	§	HARRIS COUNTY, TEXAS
	§	
PAUL RAMSEL, ET AL	§	129TH JUDICIAL DISTRICT

DEFENDANT, PAUL RAMSEL'S REQUESTS FOR PRODUCTION TO PLAINTIFF

TO: Grant Williams, Plaintiff, by and through his attorney of record, Thomas Williams, Pounds, Dale and Williams, 440 Louisiana, Suite 1400, Houston, Texas 77002.

Pursuant to Rule 196, Texas Rules of Civil Procedure, the attached requests for production are hereby propounded upon you. Said requests must be responded to separately within thirty (30) days from receipt and production of document and things responsive to said requests must be produced in the offices of the undersigned counsel within thirty (30) days from receipt of these requests.,

You are reminded that these requests for production are continuing pursuant to Rule 193.5, Texas Rules of Civil Procedure.

Respectfully submitted,

MARKS & SCHON, L.L.P.

_____
BY: Jennifer Schon
State Bar No. 1238640
4400 Pease, Suite 1100
Houston, Texas 77002
Telephone: (713) 867-5309
Facsimile: (713) 867-5308
E-Mail: schon@markschon.com

ATTORNEYS FOR DEFENDANT

18-2

IT IS HEREBY REQUESTED THAT YOU PRODUCE THE FOLLOWING DOCUMENTS AND THINGS FOR INSPECTION AND COPYING:

1.   All documents reflecting charges to Plaintiff for legal services in connection with the prosecution of this suit.

RESPONSE:

2.   All statements made by Paul Ramsel that make reference to the subject matter of this suit, including, but not limited to, writings, audiotapes, and videotapes.

RESPONSE:

3.   All written communications between you and any party to this suit that make any reference to the subject matter of this suit.

RESPONSE:

18-3

CERTIFICATE OF SERVICE

I hereby certify that a true copy of the foregoing was sent to opposing counsel by messenger on July 28, 2016.

_____
JENNIFER SCHON

ASSERTING OBJECTIONS AND PRIVILEGES

The scope of pre-trial discovery is broad. Discovery is not limited to that information that would constitute evidence at trial. Rather, the scope of discovery is that information calculated to lead to the discovery of admissible evidence. Nevertheless, there is a reasonableness standard and what constitutes reasonable discovery is normally decided by the trial judge when the parties cannot agree.

All discovery requests are subject to proper objections except Requests for Disclosure. However, objections to discovery requests must be timely and specific. Otherwise, the objection is invalid. Further, a party to a lawsuit is subject to being sanctioned by the court if objections are made without proper grounds or to interfere with legitimate discovery efforts.

Objections to discovery requests must be made on or before the date the discovery responses are due or else objections are waived. The objection must be followed by the specific grounds for the objection.

Objections to discovery requests are not ruled upon by the court unless one of the parties formally requests that the court do so. A request that a court rule on objections to discovery requests may be made before trial or during the trial. However, before a party requests that a court rule on objections, the court expects the attorneys involved to confer in an attempt to resolve the objections. If the attorneys resolve the objections, they will usually sign a Rule 11 agreement setting forth the specific terms of the resolution.

If an attorney decides that an objection to a discovery request is not reasonable, and the issue cannot be resolved with the attorney who made the objection, a **Motion to Compel Discovery** may be filed. Sometimes, the attorney making objections to discovery requests wants to obtain a ruling from the court. A **Motion for Protective Order** requests that a court rule on objectionable discovery in advance of trial.

19-1

Most objections to discovery requests fall into one of three categories:

1.   the discovery request is so unreasonable that it constitutes harassment;

2.   the discovery request imposes an undue burden upon the responding party; or

3.   the discovery request imposes an undue expense upon the responding party

The following are some examples of the proper form of objections to discovery requests:

Requests for Production:

1.   It is requested that you produce the personnel records of all persons employed by you at the time of the incident referred to in this suit, including, but not limited to applications for employment, pre-employment physical reports, performance reports and records of promotion, demotion, commendation and discipline.

> RESPONSE: OBJECTION is made to this request on the grounds that it constitutes harassment. This defendant had over 1,200 employees at the time of the incident referred to in this suit and no more than three employees of this defendant would have any personal knowledge of the incident referred to in this suit.

2.   It is requested that you produce all written complaints regarding safety with respect to the stairwell where the incident referred to in this suit occurred that were made before the incident referred to in this suit.

> RESPONSE: OBJECTION is made to this request on the grounds that it imposes an undue expense upon this defendant. The time period stated in this request is unduly broad, given the circumstances. This defendant has occupied the building where the incident referred to in this suit occurred for approximately twenty-five (25) years. In order to comply with this request, a records search through at least seven-hundred (700) boxes would

be required. This defendant contends that the cost of the search necessary to comply with this one request will be at least $5,000.

3.   It is requested that you produce all customer files for customers who requested your services during the month of the incident referred to in this suit.

RESPONSE: OBJECTION is made to this request on the grounds that it imposes an undue burden upon this defendant. The customer files requested contain specifications that may constitute trade secrets owned by the customer. To comply fully with this request would require this defendant to contact each customer and seek authority to release its file. Such a request would likely have to be scrutinized by the counsel for the customer and, if the customer refused to grant authority to release its file, or any part of the file; this defendant would face impairment of customer relations and future litigation if it turned over the customer file to the opposing party in this suit.

Students should review the following rules regarding objections:
        Rule 192.3, TRCP – Scope of Discovery
        Rule 192.4, TRCP – Limitations on Scope of Discovery
        Rule 192.6, TRCP – Protective Orders
        Rule 193.2, TRCP – Objecting to Written Discovery
        Rule 193.4, TRCP – Hearing and Ruling on Objections and Assertions of Privilege

Another problem area relating to the scope of discovery concerns the right of a party to refuse to produce information based upon an assertion of privilege. The law recognizes that certain information is privileged from disclosure. There are a number of privileges that may be asserted in litigation, but by far the two most common privileges asserted during the course of pre-trial discovery are:
        (1) attorney-client privilege; and
        (2) work product privilege.

Attorney-client privilege refers to private communications between attorney and client. This privilege includes private communications between the paralegal and the client. The privilege belongs to the client, not the attorney or paralegal.

Work product privilege is defined and explained Rule 192.5, Texas Rules of Civil Procedure. The nature, extent and limitations of this privilege are complicated, but generally, the privilege extends to the attorney's mental impressions, internal notes, discussions with insurance representatives, consultants and investigators made during or in anticipation of litigation.

At one time, assertions of privilege in Texas were made by objection. However, the rules relating to the assertion of privilege were changed in 1999. Currently, the assertion of privilege is governed by Rule 193.3, Texas Rules of Civil Procedure and paralegals should read this rule any time the issue of privilege arises during pre-trial discovery.

EXPERT WITNESSES

There are two basic types of witnesses recognized by litigation. The first type of witness is referred to as a fact witness. A fact witness is a person who has knowledge of some fact or facts relevant to a lawsuit. For example, a person who sees a motor vehicle accident would be a fact witness in a negligence suit that arose out of the accident,

The second type of witness is known as an expert witness. An expert witness is someone whose education, training and/or experience is greater than the average person in some scientific or technical discipline, or other area of expertise. Common examples of expert witness are physicians, accountants and forensic scientists. In order for expert testimony to be used at trial, the expert must establish satisfactory qualifications as to the subject matter of the testimony, the testimony must be based upon reliable criteria and the testimony must be relevant and useful to the jury in deciding some issue in the case.

The trial judges, in both federal lawsuits and Texas state lawsuits, are required to screen expert testimony to determine its relevancy and reliability before it is admitted at trial. See: **Daubert v. Merrell Dow Pharmaceuticals, 509 U.S. 579 (1993)** and **E. I. du Pont de Nemours and Co. v. Robinson, 923 S.W.2d 549 (Tex. 1995)**. When a party questions the qualifications, relevancy or reliability of an opposing party's expert in a Texas state civil case, it is referred to as a Daubert/ Robinson Challenge.

A witness may be both a fact witness and expert witness. A common example is the treating physician of a party to a personal injury case. The physician has factual knowledge as to observations made of the injured party. However, at the same time, the treating physician is an expert witness on such issues as medical diagnosis, the need for medical treatment and the injured party's prognosis.

The Texas Rules of Civil Procedure recognize two types of experts. Rule 192.7, of the Texas Rules of Civil Procedure states the following:

1. A Testifying Expert is an expert who may be called to testify as an expert witness at trial.
2. A Consulting Expert is an expert who has been consulted, retained, or specially employed by a party in anticipation of litigation or in preparation for trial, but who is not a testifying expert.

Normally, a party does not have to disclose information on a consulting expert, as this information is subject to work product privilege. However, if a testifying expert relies upon the consulting expert in forming an opinion, then the identity and work product of the consulting expert is discoverable.

There are several important discovery rules applicable to testifying experts:

Rule 194.2(f), Texas Rules of Civil Procedure, requires disclosure, without objection, of the identity, resume, bibliography, subject matter of testimony, opinions and all information reviewed and supporting the basis for opinions, with respect to each testifying expert;

Rule 195, Texas Rules of Civil Procedure, requires the Plaintiff to disclose and provide all required information about its testifying experts at least 90 days before the end of the discovery period unless otherwise ordered by the court. Defendants must disclose and provide all required information about their testifying experts at court.

Note: the end of the discovery period will vary, depending upon which discovery control plan under Rule 190 governs the suit.

Rule 195.3, 195.4, 195.5 and 195.6, Texas Rules of Civil Procedure, govern the obligations of the parties with respect to providing reports of testifying experts and producing testifying experts for deposition.

DEPOSITIONS

A **deposition** is the taking of testimony, normally in connection with a pending case. An exception to this definition is the **Deposition Before Suit,** pursuant to **Rule 202, Texas Rules of Civil Procedure,** which permits a person to petition the court to take a deposition in advance of filing a suit.

There are two common types of depositions. The first type is the **Deposition Upon Oral Examination,** pursuant to **Rule 199, Texas Rules of Civil Procedure.** Oral depositions normally involve the appearance of a party or witness before the attorneys for the parties to the suit and a court reporter. The attorneys then proceed to question the party or witness under oath. The **Deposition Upon Written Questions** pursuant to **Rule 200, Texas Rules of Civil Procedure,** differs from oral depositions. The usual purpose of depositions upon written questions is to ask limited questions to a records custodian to "prove up" business records so that the records may be admitted into evidence at trial. Normally, attorneys do not appear at depositions upon written questions. Rather, a court reporter or notary meets with the records custodian by appointment, obtains the requested records and submits standard business records questions to the custodian to be answered under oath.

Normally, written notice must be given to all parties of the intention to take a deposition. **Rules 199.2**(a) and **200.1(a), Texas Rules of Civil Procedure.** The normal practice, which is the most demanded by the trial courts, is that the parties agree to a time and place for the deposition before the written notice is issued. An oral deposition may not exceed six hours. **Rule 199.5(a), Texas Rules of Civil** Procedure. Depositions are taken under oath. **Rule 199.5(a), Texas Rules of Civil Procedure.**

Oral depositions ay be taken by stenographic means (for example, by a court reporter) or by non-stenographic means (such as a by videotape) or both. **Rule 199.1(c), Texas Rules of Civil Procedure.**

During oral depositions, only three types of objections may be made:
    (1)   objection as to the form of the question (for example, if the question calls for the witness to speculate);

(2)   objection that complains about leading the witness (when the question suggests the answer to be given); and

(3)   objection that the witness' answer was not responsive to the question asked. **Rule 199.5(e), Texas Rules of Civil Procedure.** Other objections are reserved until the time of trial.

A written deposition notice seeing to take the deposition of a party to the suit or someone under the party's control (such as an employee of the party or expert witness) has the same effect as a subpoena. Witnesses who are not parties or not under a party's control may be compelled to appear for a deposition by subpoena. **Rule 199.3, Texas Rules of Civil Procedure.**

A party or witness can be ordered to bring and produce documents and other tangible items at the time of the deposition. This is accomplished by including a request for production with the deposition notice subpoena. A request for production attached to a deposition notice or subpoena is often referred to as a duces tecum. Objections or assertions of privilege responsive to the duces tecum should normally be made at least one day before the deposition. There must be at least thirty (30) days notice for a deposition that orders production unless the parties have agreed to a shorter period or the court orders a shorter period. Otherwise, at least five (5) days notice must be given.

Depositions are versatile, often critical tools in civil litigation practice. This is especially true in the Texas state courts because they permit depositions to be used for many purposes (their uses are more limited in the federal court system). The uses of depositions in Texas state civil practice are as follows:

1.   Impeachment. If a witness' trial testimony contradicts his deposition testimony, the attorney may use the deposition to show the contradiction, either by confronting the witness in open court during cross examination or by reading the contradictory deposition to the jury;

2.   An attorney may read selected portions of a deposition aloud to a jury during trial;

3. An attorney can have someone other than the witness occupy the witness stand, as a "stand in", read questions from the deposition to the "stand in" and have the "stand in" read the answers (requires approval by the judge);

4. An attorney can edit videotaped deposition testimony and play the edits to the jury; and

5. An attorney can use deposition testimony as evidence in motions; and

6. An attorney can use deposition testimony in presentations during mediation.

Paralegals are not permitted to participate in questioning witnesses or parties in a deposition because a deposition is technically a court appearance requiring a licensed attorney. However, paralegals may attend depositions provided notice of attendance is given in accordance with **Rule 199.5(a)(3), Texas Rules of Civil Procedure.**

In addition to attending depositions, paralegals are permitted to perform a variety of important functions with respect to depositions. Some of those functions are as follows:

1. Scheduling Depositions. This is an important responsibility. The trial courts require that attorneys cooperate with each other in scheduling depositions by agreement. Trial lawyers have a multitude of trial settings, scheduled meetings and depositions in other cases and so it is usually up to the paralegals to contact all of the lawyers (and often the witness as well) and arrange a time and place that is agreeable to all. Once this is accomplished, it is then usually up to the paralegal to make sure that the appropriate deposition notices or subpoenas are issued and verify that a court reporter (and sometimes a videographer) will be in attendance;

2. Preparing for Depositions. Depositions are expensive and can be of critical importance in a case. Therefore, good preparation is essential. A busy trial lawyer takes many depositions and often it is up to the paralegal to organize documents and other information that may be used during the deposition. Further, the paralegal may assist in preparing the party or

witness for the deposition. This requires that the paralegal understand the case itself, the role that the party or witness plays in the case and deposition procedures;

3.   Summarizing Depositions. Once a deposition is completed, summaries are often prepared. Summaries are important. A 100 page deposition may yield only a few pages of critical information. By summarizing the deposition, the attorney can quickly access this critical information during other depositions. A good deposition summary requires an understanding of the legal and factual issues in a case, as well as excellent writing skills.

Given the significant involvement by paralegals in the deposition process, a few practice pointers are in order:

1.   Most depositions are taken in the conference rooms of an attorney's office, but this is not a requirement. Therefore; make sure that the specific location of the deposition will comfortably accommodate all persons attending, as wells as videotaping equipment when appropriate. This is especially important when a deposition is taken outside of the law office environment;

2.   When the deposition of a party to a suit is being taken, it is customary that the deposition be taken in the office of the party's attorney;

3.   If your firm is producing the party or witness for deposition, make sure that the party or witness is fully prepared. This includes advising the witness on directions to the location of the deposition, proper attire (especially if the witness) is appearing for a videotaped deposition), proper conduct during a deposition, and (with emphasis) that a deposition is a type of court proceeding that is under oath;

4.   Be mindful of the ethical restriction on direct contact with opposing party, employee of an opposing party or expert employed by and opposing party. Such contacts, even for the purpose of scheduling a deposition, must be through opposing counsel; and

5. On the day before each deposition, contact those persons and/or attorneys who are expected to appear at the deposition and confirm that they will be in attendance. Sometimes, depositions are scheduled over a month in advance and people forget about the deposition or fail to calendar the deposition.

Depositions are sometimes reset for a variety of reasons, including trail settings, which take precedence over depositions, illness and so forth. When a reset occurs, it is important to notify everyone involved, both by phone and in writing. Further, in the event that a deposition is reset, an amended deposition notice or subpoena should be issued.

NO. 2016-10341

GRANT WILLIAMS	§	IN THE DISTRICT COURT OF
	§	
VS.	§	HARRIS COUNTY, TEXAS
	§	
PAUL RAMSEL, ET AL	§	129TH JUDICIAL DISTRICT

NOTICE OF INTENTION TO TAKE DEPOSITION UPON ORAL EXAMINATION DUCES TECUM

TO: Grant Williams, Plaintiff, by and through his attorney of record, Thomas Williams, Pounds, Dale and Williams, 440 Louisiana, Suite 1400, Houston, Texas 77002.

Pursuant to Rule 199, Texas Rules of Civil Procedure, Defendant, Paul Ramsel, will take the deposition upon oral examination of Plaintiff, Grant Williams, at 11:00 a.m. on February 1, 2016, in the offices of Plaintiff's counsel, before Gail Sanchez, a court reporter and officer authorized to administer oaths. This deposition shall be videotaped.

The Plaintiff is hereby instructed to comply with the attached duces tecum.

Respectfully submitted,

MARKS & SCHON, L.L.P.

_____
BY: Jennifer Schon
State Bar No. 1238640
4400 Pease, Suite 1100
Houston, Texas 77002
Telephone: (713) 867-5309
Facsimile: (713) 867-5308
E-Mail: schon@markschon.com

ATTORNEYS FOR DEFENDANT

21-6

DUCES TECUM

THE WITNESS IS HEREBY INSTRUCTED TO BRING AND PRODUCE THE

FOLLOWING DOCUMENTS AND THINGS AT THE TIME OF HIS DEPOSITION:

1.   All communications passing between the Plaintiff and each Defendant to this

suit, including, but not limited to correspondence and E-mail; and

2.   All documents and writings of any kind showing the Plaintiff's communications

with potential purchasers of Customtech, Inc.

CERTIFICATE OF SERVICE

I hereby certify that a true copy of the foregoing was sent to opposing counsel by
messenger on January 8, 2016.

_____

JENNIFER SCHON

GRANT WILLIAMS	§	IN THE DISTRICT COURT OF
	§	
VS.	§	HARRIS COUNTY, TEXAS
	§	
PAUL RAMSEL, ET AL	§	129TH JUDICIAL DISTRICT

NOTICE OF INTENTION TO TAKE DEPOSITION UPON WRITTEN QUESTIONS DUCES TECUM

TO: Grant Williams, Plaintiff, by and through his attorney of record, Thomas Williams, Pounds, Dale and Williams, 440 Louisiana, Suite 1400, Houston, Texas 77002.

Pursuant to Rule 200.1, Texas Rules of Civil Procedure, that twenty (20) days after the service of copy hereof of the attached questions, a deposition upon written questions will be taken of the custodian of records for Sterling Brokerage Associates, 2211 Norfolk, Suite 225, Houston, Texas 77098 (713) 238-9708, before a representative and duly authorized Notary Public for Addendum Court Reporting, 20 Marcus Lane, Houston, Texas 77007, (281) 774-4077.

Notice is further given that request is hereby made as authorized under Rules 200 and 205 of the Rules of Civil Procedure, to the officer authorized to take this deposition to issue a subpoena duces tecum and cause it to be served upon the witness to produce the following: **records of all business transactions in which Grant Williams was the broker.**

Respectfully submitted,

MARKS & SCHON, L.L.P.

_____
BY: Jennifer Schon
State Bar No. 1238640
4400 Pease, Suite 1100
Houston, Texas 77002
Telephone: (713) 867-5309
Facsimile: (713) 867-5308
E-Mail: schon@markschon.com

ATTORNEYS FOR DEFENDANT,
PAUL RAMSEL

CERTIFICATE OF SERVICE

I hereby certify that a true copy of the foregoing was sent to opposing counsel by messenger on June 13, 2016.

_____
JENNIFER SCHON

EHIBIT A

DEPOSITION UPON WRITTEN QUESTIONS PROPOUNDED TO CUSTODIAN OF RECORDS STERLING BROKERAGE ASSOCIATES

Specifically subpoenaed are records of all business transactions in which Grant Williams was a broker.

1.   Please state your full name, occupation and business address.

ANSWER:

2.   Are the records of Sterling Brokerage Associates kept under your care, custody, supervision or control?

ANSWER:

3.   Are these records made and kept in the regular course of daily business activities by Sterling Brokerage Associates?

ANSWER:

4.   Were the entries in these records made at or near the time of the occurrence of the acts, events, conditions, opinions, or diagnoses therein or within a reasonable time thereafter?

ANSWER:

5.   Was it the regular course of business activity at the offices of Sterling Brokerage Associates for employees or representatives with personal knowledge, or who had been furnished such knowledge of acts, events, conditions, opinions, or diagnoses to make such records or to transmit information thereof to be in cluded in such records?

ANSWER:

6.   Do you have such records as described above and so described in the subpoena?

ANSWER:

7.   Was the method of preparation of these records trustworthy?

ANSWER:

8.   Please provide the officer taking this deposition photographic copies of all records set forth in the subpoena duces tecum. Have you complied?

ANSWER:

9.   Have you provided all of the records required by the subpoena duces tecum?

ANSWER:

10.   Are the records that you have provided to the officer taking this deposition accurate and complete?

ANSWER:

_____
CUSTODIAN

_____, custodian of records for Sterling Brokerage Associates, appeared before me stating that the answer to each and every question is true and that he/she has provided an exact duplicate of the original records described in the subpoena duces tecum.

SWORN TO AND SUBSCRIBED, before me on this _____, day of _____, 2016.

_____
NOTARY PUBLIC

21-11

BUSINESS RECORDS

Evidence is information that tends to prove or disprove something. One function of a court is to control what information is seen or heard by a jury. Courts seek to ensure that information presented to a jury is pertinent to the particular issues in the case (relevant and material) and that the information not be so unfairly prejudicial as to prevent a verdict based upon the relevant facts. Finally, courts seek to ensure that information presented to a jury is reliable. One reason that courts restrict admission of hearsay is because a statement of fact by a person who actually saw, heard or experienced something may be distorted when repeated by someone else. Under most circumstances, information tends to be more reliable when the individual with personal knowledge of an event or transaction testifies and is subject to cross examination.

In Texas civil cases, what information may be admitted as evidence at trial is governed by the Texas Rules of Evidence.

Paralegals are not expected to be experts in the law of evidence. However, there is one type of evidence that paralegals will encounter in civil litigation constantly and about which they must have knowledge. This type of evidence is known as business records.

Business records means records that are created in the normal course of business activity and include medical records, medical bills, employment records, records by a government agency and so forth. Virtually every case will have some type of written record offered into evidence. A written record is hearsay. However, **Rule 803(6), Texas Rules of Evidence** makes business records that are shown to be reliable admissible as an exception to the general rule against hearsay.

A written record may be rendered admissible as a business record in the following ways:

1. by agreement between the parties, such as by Rule11 agreement;
2. by admission per response to request for admission;
3. by testimony of a custodian of the records, by deposition or live at trial; or
4. by use of a business records declaration or affidavit that complies with **Rule 902(10), Texas Rules of Evidence.**

The common ways that business records are rendered admissible are by deposition upon written questions (see example in an earlier section of this book) and by business records affidavit. However, please note the following:

1. depositions upon written questions are subject to deadlines imposed by discovery control plans under Rule 190, Texas Rules of Evidence; and
2. business records and declarations affidavits must be filed with the clerk of the court at least 14 days before trial (with notice to opposing counsel) and copies of the affidavit and records filed must be made available promptly to opposing counsel. **Rule 902(10), Texas Rules of Evidence**

Please note that medical bills proven as business records are not admissible until it is shown by proper evidence that the amount of the bills are reasonable and the medical care provided was necessary. One common way to prove such bills is to have a health care provider testify that the charges reflected by the bills were reasonable and that the care was necessary. However, medical bills can also be proven to be reasonable and necessary by use of a medical bill affidavit authorized by **Section 18.001, Texas Civil Practice and Remedies Code.**

Cause No. _____

JOHN DOE	§	IN THE DISTRICT COURT
	§	
VS.	§	HARRIS COUNTY, TEXAS
	§	
MARY SMITH	§	_____ JUDICIAL DISTRICT

BUSINESS RECORDS DECLARATION

BEFORE ME, the undersigned authority, on this day personally appeared _____ who declared under penalty of perjury as follows:

"My name is _____, I am of sound mind, capable of making this declaration, and personally acquainted with the facts herein stated:

1. I am custodian of records of the records of _____ and am familiar with the manner in which its records are created and maintained by virtue of my duties and responsibilities.

2. Attached are _____ pages of records. These are the original records or exact duplicates of the original records.

3. It is the regular practice of _____ to make this type of record at or near the time of each act, event, condition, opinion, or diagnosis set forth in the record.

4. It is the regular practice of _____ for this type of record to be made by, or from information, transmitted by, persons with knowledge of the matters set forth in them.

5. It is the regular practice of _____ to keep this type of record in the course of regularly conducted business activity.

6. It is the regular practice of the business activity to make the records."

_____   _____

DECLARANT SIGNATURE   DATE

_____

PRINTED NAME OF DECLARANT

UNSWORN BUSINESS RECORDS DECLARATION AUTHORIZED BY
RULES 803(6) and 902(10), TEXAS RULES OF EVIDENCE
EFFECTIVE APRIL 1, 2015

22-3

Cause No. _____

JOHN DOE	§	IN THE DISTRICT COURT
	§	
VS.	§	HARRIS COUNTY, TEXAS
	§	
MARY SMITH	§	_____ JUDICIAL DISTRICT

BUSINESS RECORDS AFFIDAVIT

BEFORE ME, the undersigned authority, on this day personally appeared

_____, who, after being duly sworn, stated the following

"My name is _____, I am of sound mind, capable of

making this declaration, and personally acquainted with the facts herein stated:

1. I am custodian of records of the records of _____ and am familiar with

    the manner in which its records are created and maintained by virtue of my duties and responsibilities.

2. Attached are _____ pages of records. These are the original records or exact duplicates of

    the original records.

3. It is the regular practice of _____ to make this type of record at or

    near the time of each act, event, condition, opinion, or diagnosis set forth in the record.

4. It is the regular practice of _____ for this type of record to be made

    by, or from information, transmitted by, persons with knowledge of the matters set forth in them.

5. It is the regular practice of _____ to keep this type of record in the

    course of regularly conducted business activity.

6. It is the regular practice of the business activity to make the records.

_____
AFFIANT'S SIGNATURE

_____
PRINTED NAME

22-4

SWORN TO AND SUBSCRIBED before me on the _____ day of _____, 2016.

_____
NOTARY PUBLIC – STATE OF TEXAS

**BUSINESS RECORDS AFFIDAVIT AUTHORIZED
BY RULE 902, TEXAS RULES OF EVIDENCE**

Cause No. _____

JOHN DOE	§	IN THE DISTRICT COURT
	§	
VS.	§	HARRIS COUNTY, TEXAS
	§	
MARY SMITH	§	_____ JUDICIAL DISTRICT

BUSINESS RECORDS/MEDICAL BILL AFFIDAVIT

BEFORE ME, the undersigned authority, on this day personally appeared [the name of the records custodian], who, after being duly sworn, stated the following

"I am the custodian of records for [name of business]. Attached to this affidavit are [number of pages] pages of records from [name of business]. These said [number of pages] pages are kept by [name of business] in the regular course of business, and it was the regular course of business of [name of business] for an employee or representative of [name of business], with knowledge of the act, event, condition, opinion, or diagnosis, recorded to make the record was made at or near the time or reasonably soon thereafter. The records attached hereto are the original or exact duplicates of the original and are part of this affidavit. The records attached hereto include an itemized statement of the service and the charge for the service that [name of business] provided to [name of patient] on the dates indicated in the attached records. The service provided to [name of patient] on the dates indicated in the attached records. The service provided was necessary and the amount charged for the service was reasonable at the time and place the service was provided."

_____
AFFIANT'S SIGNATURE

SWORN TO AND SUBSCRIBED before me on the _____ day of _____, 2016.

_____
NOTARY PUBLIC – STATE OF TEXAS

SAMPLE BUSINESS RECORDS/MEDICAL BILL AFFIDAVIT
PURSUANT TO SECTION 18.001
TEXAS CIVIL PRACTICE AND REMEDIES CODE

MOTIONS

A motion is a request to the court for relief in connection with a pending case. The procedures with respect to presenting motions (motion practice) can vary from county to county and from court to court. Always review the local rules of the court where the suit is pending before filing a motion.

Normally, it is up to the party desiring relief from the court to file a motion. While the court can sometimes take action on its own motion (called sua sponte), the court's authority in this regard is limited.

With respect to most motions, the parties are required to "confer" before the motion is filed to determine whether the motion is contested. To aid the court, the title of the motion should reference the other party's position as to the merits of the motion. Examples are:

> "Joint Motion for Continuance"
> "Plaintiff's Agreed Motion for Continuance"
> "Plaintiff's Unopposed Motion for Continuance"
> "Plaintiff's Opposed Motion for Continuance"

Further, most motions require a "certificate of conference" in which the attorney filing the motion certifies to the court that there has been a conference on the merits of the motion.

Some courts require that the attorneys for the parties physically appear in court to argue the merits of a motion. Other courts rule on motions by submission, meaning that the attorneys will not appear and the court will rule based solely upon the documents filed by the parties.

Always review the appropriate Rules of Civil Procedure before filing a motion. Certain motions have special requirements. Examples of motions which have special requirements:

> Motion for Continuance
> Motion to Retain
> Motion to Reinstate
> Special Appearance

Motion for Default Judgment
Motion for Summary Judgment

Careful review of the Rules of Civil Procedure, the local rules and confirmation of the local practice with the clerk of the court will result in successful motion practice.

NO. 2016-10341

GRANT WILLIAMS	§	IN THE DISTRICT COURT OF
	§	
VS.	§	HARRIS COUNTY, TEXAS
	§	
PAUL RAMSEL, ET AL	§	129TH JUDICIAL DISTRICT

DEFENDANT, PAUL RAMSEL'S OPPOSED MOTION TO COMPEL DISCOVERY

COMES NOW, PAUL RAMSEL, a Defendant in above-entitled and numbered cause, moving this Court to compel discovery on the part of the Plaintiff, GRANT WILLIAMS, and in this regard would show this Court the following:

I.

This Defendant, by request for production, has sought to require the Plaintiff to produce "all writings and matter in graphic form that show the work performed by Plaintiff's attorney and the charges for said work". The Plaintiff has refused to produce documents responsive to said request on the grounds of attorney-client privilege and work product privilege.

II.

This Defendant contends that he is entitled to the information sought in its request, as the Plaintiff has sought to recover attorney's fees in this case. This Defendant is entitled to discover the basis for the attorney's fees so he can determine whether the fees requested are reasonable and necessary. Accordingly, the Court should order the Plaintiff to produce all items responsive to the request.

WHEREFORE, PREMISES CONSIDERED, this Defendant prays his motion be in all things granted and this Defendant further prays for general relief.

23-3

Respectfully submitted,

MARKS & SCHON, L.L.P.

_____
BY: Jennifer Schon
State Bar No. 1238640
4400 Pease, Suite 1100
Houston, Texas 77002
Telephone: (713) 867-5309
Facsimile: (713) 867-5308
E-Mail: schon@markschon.com

ATTORNEYS FOR DEFENDANT,
PAUL RAMSEL

CERTIFICATE OF CONFERENCE

I hereby certify that I conferred with opposing counsel regarding the merits of this motion and no agreement could be reached.

_____
JENNIFER SCHON

CERTIFICATE OF SERVICE

I hereby certify that a true copy of the foregoing was sent to opposing counsel by certified mail, return receipt requested on August 13, 2016.

_____
JENNIFER SCHON

23-4

NO. 2016-10341

GRANT WILLIAMS	§	IN THE DISTRICT COURT OF
	§	
VS.	§	HARRIS COUNTY, TEXAS
	§	
PAUL RAMSEL, ET AL	§	129TH JUDICIAL DISTRICT

NOTICE OF MOTION

PLEASE TAKE NOTICE that DEFENDANT, PAUL RAMSEL'S OPPOSED MOTION

TO COMPEL DISCOVERY will be submitte4d to the Court for ruling at 8:00 a.m. on Monday,

August 22, 2016, without an oral hearing unless one is otherwise requested by one of the parties.

Respectfully submitted,

MARKS & SCHON, L.L.P.

_____
BY: Jennifer Schon
State Bar No. 1238640
4400 Pease, Suite 1100
Houston, Texas 77002
Telephone: (713) 867-5309
Facsimile: (713) 867-5308
E-Mail: schon@markschon.com

ATTORNEYS FOR DEFENDANT,
PAUL RAMSEL

CERTIFICATE OF SERVICE

I hereby certify that a true copy of the foregoing was sent to opposing counsel by

certified mail, return receipt requested on August 16, 2016.

_____
JENNIFER SCHON

23-5

NO. 2016-10341

GRANT WILLIAMS	§	IN THE DISTRICT COURT OF
	§	
VS.	§	HARRIS COUNTY, TEXAS
	§	
PAUL RAMSEL, ET AL	§	129TH JUDICIAL DISTRICT

ORDER

On this day the Court considered DEFENDANT, PAUL RAMSEL'S OPPOSED MOTION TO COMPEL DISCOVERY. After due consideration, the motion is in all things GRANTED. It is therefore

ORDERED that the Plaintiff, GRANT WILLIAMS, produce all writings and matter in graphic form that show the work performed by the Plaintiff's attorney and the charges for said work to counsel for Defendant, PAUL RAMSEL, within ten (10) days from the date this order is signed.

Signed on this _____ day of August, 2016.

_____
JUDGE PRESIDING

APPROVED AS TO FORM AND SUBSTANCE:

MARKS & SCHON, L.L.P.

BY: _____
Jennifer Schon
State Bar No. 1238640
4400 Pease, Suite 1100
Houston, Texas 77002
Telephone: (713) 867-5309
Facsimile: (713) 867-5308
E-Mail: schon@markschon.com

ATTORNEYS FOR DEFENDANT,
PAUL RAMSEL

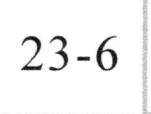

23-6

DISPOSING OF A CASE WITHOUT TRIAL

Unlike a criminal case, there is no constitutional right to a trial in a civil case. The constitutional right of **due process of law**, sometimes called **procedural due process**, means **notice** of the charge or claim and the **opportunity to be heard**. In criminal cases, due process requires a trial because the defendant is presumed innocent. However, in a civil case, there is no constitutional presumption of innocence. In a civil case, due process is fulfilled by giving the parties a **trial of disputed facts**. If there are no disputed facts, the judge can decide the case without a trial. This is called a **summary judgment**.

There are two types of summary judgment in Texas. The first type is called a **no evidence motion for summary judgment.** This type of motion for summary judgment contends that there is no evidence to support one or more of the required elements of the Plaintiff's claim. When a Defendant files such a motion, the Plaintiff must file a response with evidence establishing a prima facie case (some evidence of each of the required elements of the claim(s) asserted). This response must be filed within a specific period of time, which can be as little as fourteen days from the date the motion is filed. The second type is a **standard motion for summary judgment**. Any party can file such a motion. For this type of motion to be valid, the moving party must produce evidence and legal authority to establish:

1.   There is no material fact in dispute; and

2.   Based upon the undisputed facts, the moving party is entitled to judgment as a matter of law. The party resisting the motion must provide the court with opposing evidence and/or opposing legal authority, again usually within as little as fourteen days from the date the motion is filed.

Please note that when a party fails to respond in a timely manner to a motion for summary judgment, the motion is presumed to be valid. Therefore, one must keep in mind that motions for summary judgment are time sensitive and make sure that the attorney is aware of the response deadline to such motions.

Summary judgments in Texas state courts are governed by **Rule 166a, Texas Rules of Civil Procedure.** Anytime one is faced with a motion for summary judgment, he/she should immediately read **Rule 166a, Texas Rules of Civil Procedure.**

There are a number of other ways that civil cases in Texas may be disposed of without trial.

A **nonsuit** is a voluntary dismissal of a case. For example, if a case is settled between the parties, this is one way to close out the case.

An **involuntary dismissal** occurs when the court dismisses a case without the consent of the Plaintiff. This type of dismissal is permitted by **Rule 91a, Texas Rules of Civil Procedure.**

A **dismissal for want of prosecution (DWOP)** can occur when the Plaintiff fails to set the case for trial in a timely manner, fails to announce ready for trial at the call of the trial docket or fails to appear before trial.

A **default judgment** occurs when the Defendant fails to timely answer the lawsuits or as the result of a sanction imposed by the court.

While **judgments and dismissals** both dispose of cases, their legal effect is different. A **dismissal** disposes of a case without deciding the merits of a case. There are two types of dismissals. A **dismissal without prejudice** means that the Plaintiff may refile the case at some later point, subject to the **statute of limitations.** A d**ismissal with prejudice** means that the Plaintiff may not refile the case.

A **judgment** is a legal decision in a case that decides the merits of a case. In this regard, it is important to note that a verdict, which refers to the factual findings in a case (usually by a jury), does not conclude a case. Rather, the verdict must be translated into a legal decision - namely a judgment. In order for a judgment to completely dispose of a case, it must dispose of all claims by all parties to the case. This is called a final judgment. Once there is a **final judgment,** the case cannot be refiled because of the rule against re-litigation of final judgments called res judicata. Sometimes a judgment does not dispose of all claims by all parties to the case. This is called an **interlocutory judgment.**

OTHER PRE-TRIAL MATTERS

Pre-Trial Orders

In both the Texas state civil courts and the federal courts, the individual judges have discretion with respect to the organization of cases scheduled for trial. Some judges issue pre-trial orders in which the parties are required to provide certain information in an organized fashion before the time of trial. While there are variations from court to court, generally the format is similar. Most pre-trial orders require that the parties provide the following:

1.   the names of the parties and their counsel;
2.   a brief description of the nature of the case;
3.   a list of the undisputed facts in the case;
4.   a list of the factual contentions of each party to the case;
5.   the legal authority applicable to the case;
6.   a list of the fact and expert witnesses for each party;
7.   marked exhibits to be offered by each party at trial;
8.   a list of those sections of depositions, by page and line number, that the parties intend to offer at trial;
9.   the motion in limine by each party;
10.   the proposed jury charge by each party [proposed definitions, instructions and questions to be presented to the jury]

The court's web site and local rules to determine whether or not the judge requires a pre-trial order. If one is required, the judge will normally specify the content of the pre-trial order and when it is due.

Alternative Dispute Resolution (ADR)

During the mid 1980's, the Texas state courts began to experiment with methods to encourage settlement between the parties in civil suits. Settlement is a preferred method to resolve civil suits because the parties to the suit control their own destiny by voluntary settlement and it also saves time and expense, both for the parties to the suit and the court system. The courts reasoned that in some cases, the parties became so polarized and adversarial that they would not initiate settlement efforts. After a period of study and experimentation, it was determined that court ordered

mediation was an effective settlement tool. The Texas legislature passed a statute that gave the Texas state trial judges the power to order mediation in civil cases. Mediation is a settlement negotiation process that uses a disinterested third person to guide the process. This disinterested third person, called a mediator, moves back and forth between the parties, presenting settlement proposals and counter proposals while the parties are in separate rooms in the same office. The mediator only discloses information authorized by the parties, but encourages the parties to explain the reasons for their attitudes about the case, as well as the strengths and weaknesses of their positions in the case. Often, the mediator will guide the parties to a settlement. Due to the success of mediation in the resolution of cases, the courts often order the parties to mediate. The mediators are usually experienced attorneys and retired or former judges.The mediation process works as follows:

1. the parties to the suit and their attorneys appear together in a conference room in the presence of the mediator. The mediator obtains a verbal commitment from each party to attempt in good faith to settle the case;

2. while the parties, attorneys and mediator are still together, the attorneys for each party makes a presentation. The mediator may ask questions during the presentation;

3. the opposing parties, along with their attorneys, are placed in separate rooms and the mediator begins moving back and forth between the sides, attempting to obtain settlement proposals and counter proposals;

4. if the parties settle, a basic settlement agreement is signed. More formal settlement documents will be signed at a later date. If the parties cannot reach settlement, it is called an impasse. Typically, mediation is scheduled for one half day or an entire day. However, the parties can agree to extend the time of mediation. The cost of the mediator is usually shared by the parties

5. the mediator notifies the court as to the success or failure of the mediation.

Mediation is a confidential process and what is said during the mediation cannot be used as evidence. Further, the mediator may not be a witness or source of evidence in the case.

Paralegals are permitted to appear at mediation. Further, they often work with the attorney to prepare for the mediation. Since there are few specific requirements to be followed in mediation, lawyers tend to prepare for the process differently. However, since mediation is a costly process [$500 to $1,500 per day per party] and because it is often successful, most attorneys prepare extensively for the process. One important role for the paralegal at mediation is comforting the client. All legal processes tend to be unfamiliar to most clients and they are often uncomfortable and intimidated. Often, it is comforting to have someone to talk to during the inevitable waiting that is part of the mediation process.

THE PARALEGAL AND THE TRIAL

The trial has evolved in America to the point that it is considered by some to be a popular art form. Simply stated, Americans are fascinated by the trial as a real life type of drama. American fascination with trials is nothing new. From the trial of Aaron Burr for treason in the early 1800's to the O.J. Simpson murder trial in the 1990's, the fact is, Americans love a good high profile trial. Indeed, this fascination with high profile trials has even led to a cable television network devoted to the televising and analysis of such trials. While most high profile trials are criminal trials, the civil trial is getting more and more attention. This recent interest in civil trials appears to be connected with the popularity of reality television that emerged in the late 1990's.

The truth about trials, especially from those who put them together and try them, is quite a bit different from their popular image. A trial is a presentation of conflicting versions of facts and the impressions that should be drawn from the facts, by adversary parties. This presentation, which is normally made by lawyers, is made to strangers to the facts of the case – namely a judge and jury.

A trial cannot be perfectly scripted by any lawyer, because witnesses are subject to cross-examination by the opposing lawyer and the admissibility of all evidence is subject to challenge by the opposing lawyer and review by the judge. The mission of the trial lawyer is to create the greatest degree of predictability in the presentation of the client's case, while legally and ethically disrupting the ability of the opposing party to present a contrary version of the facts and theme of the case.

It would be nice to say that a good lawyer does not matter, but instead what really matters is the truth, virtue and what is ultimately right. However, such is just not the case. Why? Because often what is true or right depends upon one's perspective and opinion, and because decent people often draw differing conclusions from the same set of facts. How the facts are presented can have a lot to do with the conclusions that are drawn by strangers to the facts – again, a judge and jury. Therefore, a good trial lawyer can make a difference in the outcome of a case.

What makes an excellent trial lawyer? After all, excellent trial lawyers can be male or female, any race or ethnicity, tall, short, thick, thin and so forth. The answer is preparation and experience – and the paralegal can be absolutely essential to the preparation of a case for trial. Indeed, most cases are won or lost before trial due preparation. This is especially true in civil cases, which usually have much more pre-trial discovery than criminal cases.

Most paralegal work in civil litigation occurs before trial. This makes sense as most civil cases are resolved without trial, by settlement. However, inevitably, some cases will go to trial and the paralegal can expect to be performing some very critical functions just before and during trial.

Just Before Trial.

1. Preparation of Motion in Limine. This motion, which is often presented and ruled upon just before trial, seeks to prevent an opposing counsel from mentioning certain matters in the presence of the jury. The purpose of this motion is to prevent objectionable and prejudicial matters from being mentioned during the trial by obtaining a court order before the trial. The matters that will be sought to be excluded by an order in limine will vary from case to case. Further, attorneys are usually very particular about their motions in limine. A paralegal should make sure and have an acceptable draft format of such a motion in the computer just in case the lawyer is suddenly ordered to appear for trial;

2. Contacting clients and witnesses. It is rare that any litigant can be certain as to when a case will go to trial. Most of the time, cases are set for a term of court. This means that the case is subject to go to trial during a particular one-week, two-week or one-month period. Many cases are often set for the same term of court, so that if cases settle, other cases will be available for trial. The cases that do not go to trial during the term will be reset for another term. The point is that a trial lawyer can never be sure when a case will go to trial. Therefore, once there is a call from the court that the parties are to appear at a specific time for trial, there is usually very little notice -sometimes as little as

a few hours. The paralegal will often be tasked to notify the clients and witnesses;

3.   Organizing the File. Yes, it should already be organized, but sometimes lawyers want the file organized differently for trial than it was during the pre-trial stage of the case;

4.   Moving file and equipment to the courtroom. This situation is highly variable from case to case. In some cases, it is necessary to move video equipment to the courtroom so arrangements can be made to show excerpts of videotaped depositions. Sometimes, charts and diagrams on hardboard need to be delivered and set up in the courtroom. Other times, the file itself may be so large that arrangements need to be made to transport it to the courtroom.

5.   Et cetera. This means be prepared for just about anything else that comes up.

During Trial

How lawyers utilize paralegals during trial depends upon many factors, including the type of case, the length and complexity of the trial and so forth. Some lawyers may want paralegals in the courtroom during the trial, while other instances want the paralegals in the office during trial. What can be stated with certainty is this: in most trials, the role of the paralegal will be one of logistics. This includes making sure the witnesses know when to appear at the courthouse to testify and dealing with emergencies that come up during the course of the trial.

Due to the important support role of paralegals just before and during trial, it is important that paralegals learn the stages of a trial, which are set forth in the next section.

THE STAGES OF A CIVIL TRIAL

1. **Voir Dire**
    The questioning of potential jurors to determine their qualifications. In Texas state court, this questioning is conducted by both the attorneys and the judge. In federal court, it is conducted by the judge, although the attorneys can submit questions that the attorneys want asked by the judge.

    Comment:
    > The attorneys can assert two types of challenges to a potential juror. The first type of challenge is called a challenge for cause, in which the attorney asserts that the potential juror is legally disqualified for a specific reason, such as bias. The second type of challenge is called the peremptory challenge, which is a challenge for no stated reason. Each party to the case usually has a specific number of this type of challenge. While no stated reason is required for this type of challenge, it cannot be used specifically dilute the racial, ethnic or gender of the jury.

    > Once the challenges have been decided, the first six or twelve of the remaining potential jurors (depending upon the particular court) in numerical order will be empaneled and sworn as the jury.

2. **Opening Statements**
    Brief statements by the attorneys for the parties as to what they believe the evidence in the case will show or prove.

    Comment:
    > The Plaintiff goes first. The Defendant can either immediately follow the Plaintiff or can wait until just before the beginning of when the defendant's case is presented.

27-1

3. **Plaintiff's Case in Chief**
The presentation of evidence by the plaintiff.

Comment:
> The plaintiff must by the evidence establish the prima facie case, which means that the plaintiff must put on some evidence of each and every required element of the cause(s) of action and remedies asserted. If the plaintiff fails to establish the prima facie case, the court will not permit the jury to decide the case, but will instead dispose of the case by directed verdict.

4. **Defendant's Case**
The presentation of evidence by the defendant.

Comment:
> The defendant is not required to present evidence, but has the right to do so. Note that while the defendant is not required to disprove the plaintiff's case in chief, the defendant does have the obligation to put on evidence of any affirmative defense that is asserted.

5. **Plaintiff's Rebuttal**
The presentation of evidence by the plaintiff limited to only that evidence that would contradict evidence presented by the defendant.

Comment:
> Because the plaintiff has the burden to establish the prima facie case, the plaintiff presents evidence first arid sometimes gets the last word by rebuttal.

6. **Charge Conference**
A conference between the attorneys and judge regarding what definitions, instructions and questions will be presented by the judge to the jury.

Comment:
> Typically, the attorneys present proposed definitions, instructions and questions to the judge and then the judge decides what will be presented to the jury.

7. **Judge "Charges" The Jury**

The judge reads the definitions, instructions and questions to the jury.

Comment:

> The term charge means the definitions, instructions and questions given by the judge to the jury. The charge, in written form, is also given to the jury to take into the jury deliberation room at the time of deliberations.

8. **Closing Statements [Final Arguments]**

The attorneys assert how the questions contained in the charge should be answered based upon the evidence in the case.

9. **Jury Deliberation**

The jury meets in secret deliberation to decide their answers to the jury questions.

Comment:

> In Texas state trial court, a jury verdict can be reached by ten jurors in a twelve person jury and five jurors in a six person jury. In other words, a unanimous verdict is not required in Texas state civil suits.

10. **Verdict**

The factual findings of the jury, namely the jury's answers to the questions in the jury are published (read in open court).

Comment:

> While the verdict concludes the trial, it does not end the case. A case that is tried is not completed until a judgment is issued by the judge.

TRIAL TERMINOLOGY

VENIRE - the panel of potential jurors from which a trial jury is chosen.

VOIR DIRE - the interrogation of potential jurors to determine their qualifications.

PEREMPTORY CHALLENGE (or peremptory strike) - challenging a potential juror for no specified reason. Each party to a suit receives a specified number of such challenges.

CHALLENGE FOR CAUSE - challenging a potential juror based upon a specified disqualifying factor.

PETIT JURY - a trial jury.

BENCH TRIAL - a trial by judge alone in which the judge decides both the facts and the law in the case.

BATSON RULE - a rule of constitutional law that holds that a peremptory challenge cannot be used for the sole purpose of excluding minorities from the jury.

TRIAL - a government sanctioned proceeding to determine the rights of parties in a particular case.

JUDGE - an official of the judicial branch of government who is responsible for conducting trials and other proceedings in accordance with law.

DAUBERT/ROBINSON CHALLENGE - a challenge of an expert witness, alleging either a lack of expert qualifications or a proper basis for expert opinion.

OPENING STATEMENT - a stage of a trial in which the attorneys summarize for the jury what they believe the evidence will show.

PRIMA FACIE CASE - refers to the obligation of a plaintiff (or prosecution in a criminal case) to produce some evidence of each required element of a claim (or crime) during the case in chief.

Note: if the plaintiff fails to make the prima facie case, then the judge will issue a directed verdict in favor of the defendant.

EVIDENCE - information which tends to prove or disprove something.

TESTIMONIAL EVIDENCE - spoken evidence from the witness stand.

PHYSICAL EVIDENCE - documents and tangible things.

DEMONSTRATIVE EVIDENCE - evidence that demonstrates a particular point, such as charts, graphs, video re-enactments and the like.

CIRCUMSTANTIAL EVIDENCE - information that does not directly prove a fact, but which may create the inference of a fact. For example: John testifies that he saw Joe rob a liquor store. This is direct evidence. Consider this, however: A liquor store is robbed and no one can identify the robber. However, Joe's driver's license is found on the floor of the liquor store -right where the robber stood -immediately after the robbery. This is circumstantial evidence.

COURT CHARGE - the definitions, instructions and questions submitted by the judge to the jury.

MOTION IN LIMINE - a motion made before trial to prevent parties, witnesses and attorneys from making reference to certain matters in the presence of the jury during a trial unless permission is first obtained by the judge. The motion prevents prejudicial information from being heard by the jury.

MOTION TO EQUALIZE PEREMPTORY CHALLENGES - a motion made before trial to fairly equalize the number of peremptory challenges in lawsuits where there are more defendants than plaintiffs or vice versa.

REBUTTAL - the right of the plaintiff (or prosecution in a criminal case) to put on evidence after the defense rests to contradict evidence presented by the defense.
THE "RULE" - refers to an order by the trial judge that witnesses cannot listen to the testimony of other witnesses during trial and may not discuss testimony with other witnesses during the trial. To obtain this order, a party to the case must ''invoke the rule''.

PREDICATE - refers to the requirements that must be met before a particular item of evidence may be admissible.

VERDICT - the factual findings in a case, usually made by a jury.

JUDGMENT - a legal decision by a judge on the merits of a case.

DECREE - means the same thing as 'judgment", except that decree usually refers to a decision made in equity.

SUBPOENA - a court order compelling a person to appear before a tribunal and give testimony.

INSTANTER - a term often used in connection with a subpoena which commands the witness to appear immediately to give testimony.

BILL OF EXCEPTION - a method of preserving a record for appeal when evidence is excluded, which involves offering the evidence outside of the presence of the jury for the limited purpose of making a record of what evidence was excluded. This practice is sometimes referred to as making a bill.

BAILIFF - an officer of the court responsible for courtroom security, summoning wit nesses to take the stand during hearings and trial, and proper sequestration of the jury.

COURT REPORTER - an officer of the court responsible for the record of official proceedings.

CLERK OF THE COURT - an officer of the court responsible for court administration.'

DOCKET - refers to the group of cases pending before a particular court.

TRIAL COORDINATOR - an officer of the court responsible for managing the court's docket.

FEDERAL COURTS AND JURISDICTION

Jurisdiction

The United States Constitution (Article III) ordered the creation of the United States Supreme Court and authorized the Congress to create such inferior courts as it deemed necessary. Under the command and authority of the Constitution, the federal court system first has three basic types of courts:

United States Supreme Court -it is the highest appeals court within the federal court system and the highest court of all American courts in deciding the meaning of the Constitution. This means that a state court case can be appealed to the United States Supreme Court if it involves an issue regarding the meaning of the United State Constitution.

United States Courts of Appeals -this is a federal appeals court that has various circuits throughout the United States.

United States District Court -this is the federal trial court and it hears both criminal and civil cases. There are numerous federal district courts throughout the United States and its territories.

Judges in the above-referenced courts are nominated by the President and must be approved by a majority of the Senate. Once these judges are approved, they can serve for life.

There are lesser federal courts, such as the bankruptcy courts, tax courts and the military courts. These courts exist for the purpose of adjudicating specialized issues of law and the judges do not have lifetime appointments.

Federal criminal subject matter jurisdiction is limited to violations of federal criminal statutes. Federal civil subject matter jurisdiction is a bit more complicated, and is as follows:

> (1) federal question jurisdiction - authority over civil cases that involve the U.S. Constitution, federal statutes or federal regulations, as well as admiralty or maritime cases (cases in volving seagoing vessels in navigable waters);

(2)   diversity of citizenship jurisdiction - authority over civil suits between citizens of different states; and

(3)   ancillary or pendent jurisdiction - authority over civil suits that involve both federal and state claims.

Civil suits that do not meet at least one of the three criteria cannot be brought in the federal courts. Rather, such cases must be brought in the state courts.

Removal

Some lawsuits can only be filed in federal court. In such cases, it is said that the federal court has exclusive jurisdiction. However, there are some lawsuits that can be filed in either federal court or state court. When a suit can be filed in either state or federal court, it is said that the courts have concurrent jurisdiction. If a suit is filed in state court, and the federal court also has jurisdiction, the person sued has the right of removal. This means that the defendant can have the suit removed from the state court to the federal court. Once such a case is removed to federal court, it will normally be decided by the federal court. However, if the plaintiff contends that there is no federal jurisdiction over a removed case and it is determined that the federal court does not have jurisdiction, the case will be remanded back to state court.

FEDERAL PROCEDURE - DIFFERENCES IN TERMINOLOGY AND PRACTICE

TERM/TEXAS STATE PRACTICE	TERM/FEDERAL PRACTICE
Plaintiff's Original Petition	Complaint - Rule 3, FRCP
Answer may be by general denial - Rule 92, TRCP	As to each allegation in complaint, must admit, deny or explain why the allegation cannot be admitted or denied. Rule 8(b), FRCP
Service of Process of Petition required	Defendant has duty to avoid the necessity of being served and waive service. Rule 4(d), FRCP
Citation	Summons
Time to answer suit in district or county court is by the first Monday following 20 days after service by 10:00 a.m.	Must answer complaint within 60 days of when waiver of service request is sent if waiver signed and returned or 20 days from service if service is necessary.
Amendment of petition or answer may be done without permission of the court as little as eight days before trial (as a practical matter must usually be 31 days before trial or by court ordered deadline to amend) as long as amendment would not delay trial due to surprise	Normally, court approval is required for amendment.
Special Exceptions (based upon vagueness)	Motion for More Definite Statement
Special Exceptions (fail to state legal claim)	Motion for Involuntary Dismissal
No Evidence Motion for Summary Judgment	Motion for Involuntary Dismissal
Requests for Disclosure	Rule 26, FRCP
Depositions may be used at trial to impeach (contradict).to refresh memory or as direct evidence	Use of depositions at trial limited per Rule 32, FRCP, to impeach and not as direct evidence unless witness is dead or otherwise not available

30-1

UNITED STATES DISTRICT COURT
FOR THE SOUTHERN DISTRICT OF TEXAS
HOUSTON DIVISION

ANNE STEVENS, PLAINTIFF   §
                                      §

VS.   §   CIVIL ACTION NO. H-16-827
                                      §

HRM, INC., DEFENDANT   §

COMPLAINT

      ANNE STEVENS, Plaintiff, complains of and against HRM, INC., Defendant, and shows this Court the following:

1.   The Court has federal question subject matter jurisdiction pursuant to 42 U.S.C., Section 2000e, et seq.

2.   Defendant, an employer with over fifteen (15) employees, hired the Plaintiff as a clerk on January 28, 2015.

3.   Plaintiff ceased her employment with Defendant on August 31, 2015.

4.   The Plaintiff's immediate supervisor during her entire period of employment with Defendant was Bill Epps, Vice President of Operations.

5.   On March 21, 2015, Bill Epps asked Plaintiff out on a date for what Epps described as "a romantic dinner to be followed by a real work out". Plaintiff refused the invitation.

6.   On April 17, 2015, Bill Epps presented Plaintiff with flowers and again asked Plaintiff out on a date. Once again, the Plaintiff refused the invitation. Epps' then asked Plaintiff, "Do you have something against men"?

7.   On April 25, 2015, Bill Epps again asked Plaintiff out on a date and again, the Plaintiff refused. Epps responded by stating that he was patient, but that someday, he would hold her in his arms. Plaintiff told Epps that she did not want to date him and requested that he not ask her out again.

31-1

8. On May 4, 2015, Plaintiff was instructed by Epps to report to his office and Plaintiff reported to his office as instructed. Plaintiff was told by Epps that he had planned to recommend Plaintiff for a raise, but that Plaintiff had failed to show him the "necessary degree of loyalty". Epps went on to state, "You will get that raise if and when you learn to show me some appreciation. Get it?"

9. On May 9, 2015, Plaintiff requested a meeting with Byron Steele, who was Epps' immediate supervisor and President of the defendant company. Plaintiff set forth the various events involving Epps' behavior towards Plaintiff. Steele's reply was, "Don't worry about Bill. He fancies himself a real ladies' man, but deep down he is harmless.

10. On June 1, 2015, Epps told Plaintiff that "… women who don't like men do not have much of a future here."

11. On June 11, 2015, Epps told Plaintiff that she should consider looking for a new job. When Plaintiff asked Epps why she should look for another job, he stated, "You work well with others, but you don't play well with others."

12. On June 12, 2015, Plaintiff again met with Steele, about Epps. Steele advised Plaintiff that Epps was Plaintiff's supervisor and that the company would abide by personnel decisions made by Epps.

13. Based upon statements made by Epps and Steele, Plaintiff began looking for a new job. Plaintiff found new employment on August 13, 2015. Plaintiff gave the Defendant a two-week notice and ceased her employment with Defendant on August 31, 2015.

14. Plaintiff's new job paid $4,000 less per year than her job with Defendant.

15. On September 15, 2015, Plaintiff filed a sexual harassment complaint against Defendant with the EEOC. The EEOC gave the Plaintiff a written notice that she was granted the right to sue Defendant on December 30, 2015.

31-2

16. Plaintiff asserts that the Defendant is liable for quid pro quo sexual harassment in violation of Title VII of the 1964 Civil Rights Act, as amended.

17. Plaintiff seeks recovery of back pay, front pay, compensation for mental anguish, attorney's fees and punitive damages.

Respectfully submitted

_____

PHILLIP SMITH, Attorney in Charge
Federal Bar ID Number 3470
1111 Fannin, Suite 4100
Houston, Texas 77002
Telephone: (713) 222-5555
Facsimile: (713) 222-4444
E-mail: pa@phillipsmithatty.com

UNITED STATES DISTRICT COURT
FOR THE SOUTHERN DISTRICT OF TEXAS
HOUSTON DIVISION

ANNE STEVENS, PLAINTIFF   §

§

VS.   §   CIVIL ACTION NO. H-16-827

§

HRM, INC., DEFENDANT   §

ANSWER

HRM, Defendant, answers the Plaintiff's complaint as follows:

1.   Responding to paragraph 1 of the complaint, the Defendant does not dispute the subject matter jurisdiction of this court.

2.   Defendant admits paragraph 2 of the complaint.

3.   Defendant admits paragraph 3 of the complaint.

4.   Defendant admits paragraph 4 of the complaint.

5.   Defendant admits that portion of paragraph 5 of the complaint in which it is stated that Epps asked Plaintiff out on a date and that Plaintiff refused. Defendant denies the remainder of paragraph 5 of the complaint.

6.   The Defendant denies all of paragraph 6 of the complaint except that it admits that Epps presented the Plaintiff with flowers on the date alleged.

7.   The Defendant denies all of paragraph 7 of the complaint.

8.   The Defendant denies all of paragraph 8 of the complaint except that it is admitted that there was a meeting between Epps and the Plaintiff on the date alleged.

9.   The Defendant denies paragraph 9 of the complaint.

10.   The Defendant denies paragraph 10 of the complaint.

11.   The Defendant denies paragraph 11 of the complaint.

12.   The Defendant admits paragraph 12 of the complaint.

13. The Defendant denies all of paragraph 13 of the complaint with the exception that it admits that the Plaintiff gave Defendant a two-week notice and ceased her employment with Defendant on August 31, 2015.

14. The Defendant has insufficient information to admit or deny paragraph 14 of the complaint.

15. The Defendant admits paragraph 15 of the complaint.

16. The Defendant denies paragraph 16 of the complaint.

17. The Defendant denies that Plaintiff is entitled to the relief sought in paragraph 17 of complaint.

Respectfully submitted

_____

DANA MILLS,

Attorney in Charge for Defendant
Federal Bar ID Number 3210
1717 Waldrop Street
Houston, Texas 77099
Telephone: (713) 789-7999
Facsimile: (713) 789-8999
E-mail: dana@millsdana.com

CERTIFICATE OF SERVICE

I hereby certify that a true and correct copy of the foregoing was sent to opposing counsel by messenger on March 28, 2016.

_____

DANA MILLS

32-2

FEDERAL PRE-TRIAL DISCOVERY

Federal civil practice is governed by the **Federal Rules of Civil Procedure**, the **Federal Rules of Evidence** and the local rules of the federal district courts.

The federal rules pertaining to discovery requests are similar to the Texas rules in that there are requests for admissions, interrogatories and requests for production. However, the federal rules do not provide for requests for disclosure. Rather, disclosure in federal civil cases is governed by **Rule 26, Federal Rules of Civil Procedure** and reading this rule carefully is essential to proper pre-trial discovery conduct. In Texas state practice, the obligation to disclose information usually requires that a request be made in writing pursuant to **Rule 194, Texas Rules of Civil Procedure.**

Rule 26, Federal Rules of Civil Procedure, requires disclosure without a request being made. Further, what must be disclosed, while similar is not exactly the same. For example, **Rule 26(a)(2)(B), Federal Rules of Civil Procedure**, requires disclosure of the testimonial history of expert witnesses. **Further, Rule 26(a)(3), Federal Rules of Civil Procedure**, requires disclosure of fact witnesses, witnesses who will be presented by deposition and exhibits that will be offered at trial.

Another difference between federal practice and Texas state practice concerns the use of pre-trial conferences involving the trial judge and attorneys for the parties. Such pre-trial conferences are generally rare in Texas state practice, while common in federal practice. Further, under the rules of federal practice, the attorneys for the parties are required to confer at least twenty one days before a scheduling conference regarding claims, defenses, settlement and other issues and attempt to develop a pre trial discovery timetable. See: **Rule 26(t), Federal Rules of Civil Procedure**.

Finally, it is generally true that federal judges exert more authority over the pretrial discovery process than do most Texas state judges. There is no rule granting federal judges greater pre-trial discovery authority than Texas state judges. Rather, it is just a fact of life. The reasons for this difference are many. One reason for the difference is that a federal trial judge usually has a staff, including a secretary and at least one attorney. Some federal trial judges have assistant judges, called U S. Magistrates, available to assist in the management of cases. On the other hand, Texas state trial judges rarely have secretaries or attorneys to assist them. Therefore, the lack of resources often limits their ability to be more directly involved in over seeing the development of cases.

Most law firms that engage in civil litigation practice in both the state and federal courts. Therefore, litigation paralegals need to be familiar with both systems.

**UNITED STATES DISTRICT COURT
FOR THE SOUTHERN DISTRICT OF TEXAS
HOUSTON DIVISION**

ANNE STEVENS, PLAINTIFF	§	
	§	
VS.	§	CIVIL ACTION NO. H-16-827
	§	
HRM, INC., DEFENDANT	§	

**PLAINTIFF'S INITIAL DISCLOSURES TO DEFENDANT
PURSUANT TO RULE 26(a)(1), FRCP**

Name, Address and Telephone Number/Persons Likely to Have Discoverable Information

1.   Anne Stevens, Plaintiff

      5251 Markview Lane

      Houston, Texas 77051

      Phone (713) 433-3448

      *Plaintiff, who would have background information on her employment at HRM, the harassment to which she was subjected and the damages she sustained.

2.   The following HRM, Inc. personnel:

      a.   Bill Epps, Vice-President of Operations [Phone: (281) 486-2601]

            *Was Plaintiff's supervisor, who harassed her.

      b.   Byron Steele, President [Phone: (281) 486-2600]

            *Has knowledge that Plaintiff reported Epps' harassment to him and that no action was taken.

      c.   Arlese J. Hall, Administrative Clerk [Phone (281) 486-288]

            *Heard Epps ask Plaintiff out on a date – heard Plaintiff refuse – heard Epps ask Plaintiff whether she disliked men.

34-1

3.	Gloria Revson, M.D.

	400 Westheimer

	Houston, Texas 77006

	Phone: (713) 523-6000

	*Psychiatrist who has been treating the Plaintiff and who began treating the Plaintiff while the Plaintiff was at HRM. Will testify as to psychic injuries sustained by the Plaintiff as a result of the harassment and the reasonable cost of necessary psychiatric care.

4.	Philip Smith

	Attorney at Law

	1111 Fannin, Suite 4100

	Houston, Texas 77002

	Phone: (713) 222-5555

	*Will testify as to reasonable and necessary attorney's fees with respect to the prosecution of the Plaintiff's suit.

**Note:	the Plaintiff gives notice that the above referenced persons/entities are expected to be called to testify at trial. Rule 26(a)(3)(A) FRCP**

Documents/Tangible Things/Electronically Stored Information (ESI)

1.	HRM personnel records on Plaintiff (attached);

2.	Vulgar e-mail to Plaintiff from Epps dated April 20, 2015 (attached);

3.	Psychiatric records/bills pertaining to treatment of Plaintiff by Gloria Revson M.D. (attached);

4.	EEOC Compliant by Plaintiff against HRM, Inc. (attached);

5.	"Right to Sue" Letter issued by EEOC (attached);

6.	Billing statement by Phillip Smith, Attorney (attached);

7.	Plaintiff's federal tax returns for 2012-2015.

Computation of Damages

1. Loss of income – $2,000 for three weeks it took to find new job and $8,000 in reduction in earnings because new job paid less than HRM, per tax returns and employment records;

2. Psychiatric Care – $2,500 – past care and $14,000 in future care, per Dr. Revson's records and bills;

3. Mental Anguish: Plaintiff and Dr. Revson will testify as to this element of damage. The Plaintiff is seeking $150,000 in mental anguish damage;

4. Attorney's fees – this will be proven by the billing records and testimony by Plaintiff's attorney – attorney's fees to date are $25,500, based upon a $250 hourly rate.

Insurance Agreements

These documents are in the possession of the Defendant.

Respectfully submitted

_____

PHILLIP SMITH, Attorney in Charge
Federal Bar ID Number 3470
1111 Fannin, Suite 4100
Houston, Texas 77002
Telephone: (713) 222-5555
Facsimile: (713) 222-4444
E-mail: pa@phillipsmithatty.com

CERTIFICATE OF SERVICE

I hereby certify that a true copy of the foregoing was hand-delivered to the office of the counsel for the Defendant on April 13, 2016.

_____

PHILLIP SMITH

34-3

INNOVATIONS – STATE AND FEDERAL

Introduction

Your author's career in law began in October, 1971, as a paralegal student/trainee in a military legal office. My first experience with "keyboarding" was on a manual typewriter and the IBM Selectric typewriter was considered high science. Making "copies" was done using "carbon paper" between the original document in the typewriter and other pieces of paper that were also in the typewriter. After a year typing on a manual typewriter, my fingers were so strong, I wondered if I had a future as a martial artist.

There are two uncompromising forces that affect the law: technology and evolution of social behavior. Both of these forces have been "on fire" during the last thirty-five years. Consider just a few of the onslaught of "new things" that have necessitated substantial changes in the law:

1. phones to mobile phones to camera phones to smart phones;
2. PC's, desktops, laptops, "pads"
3. e-mails, voice mails, text mails, tweets and so on and so on;
4. broadband and wi-fi;
5. social media and its "anti-matter" – privacy rights;
6. the Internet;
7. the ATM and electronic banking;
8. the LGBT revolution;
9. the revolution in non-invasive and minimally invasive diagnosis and treatment;
10. electronic commerce;
11. electronic "currency" such as "bitcoin";
12. hacking and other computer based criminal activity;
13. DNA and CSI;
14. "drones"; and
15. so on and so on and Pokemon Go.

Please note not only do the "new things" often lead to civil litigation in order to resolve "new" disputes, but leads to major changes in the law of civil procedure and evidence. This section notes some of the innovations that have had a significant impact upon the practice of civil litigation.

This section notes some of the innovations that have had a significant impact upon the practice of civil litigation.

"Formulary Practice"

As a law student, the author of this book did not aspire to be a lawyer, but instead to become a trial lawyer. This aspiration was akin to wanting to be a fighter pilot instead of a pilot. As the reader has probably figured out, the author suffered from too much Perry Mason and not enough maturity. Fortunately, becoming a trial lawyer preceded becoming a grown up and the rest is history.

Becoming a trial lawyer is a challenging process and this process ideally begins with aspiring trial lawyer working at the direction of an experienced trial lawyer.

One skill that an aspiring trial lawyer traditionally had to develop was the customized drafting of the lawsuit and related documents. The lawyer's name and signature is on these documents and traditionally, poorly drafted documents made one wonder about the quality of the lawyer. Traditionally, if a lawyer was poor at drafting documents then it was prudent to employ a skilled legal secretary.

Today, customized drafting of lawsuits and related documents are becoming a thing of the past. Instead, "formulary" systems such as "ProDoc" provides thousands of litigation formats and transactional document formats (such as contracts, corporate documents and so forth) which permits the attorney to draft documents by responding to "prompts" and then "editing" the form that is produced. Often, such systems are online which allows for immediate modification of the forms if laws change. Such systems are akin to cable television in that the lawyer is charged based upon the scope of the services chosen by the lawyer. Using a formulary system typically saves time and money and such systems are here to stay.

Given the incredible mobility of laptop computers and wi-fi access, documents can be easily created outside of the office.

Paralegals

The practice of law began in Rome, which had evolved into both a military and a commercial empire. In time, there were lawyers, law schools and courts. In addition, there were non-lawyers who assisted the lawyers known in the Roman system as scribes and later known in Europe as scriveners. Until approximately 1900 virtually all legal documents were handwritten by them. With the invention of the typewriter came the

legal secretary, a non-lawyer trained in shorthand and use of the typewriter. Those non-lawyer professionals, other than legal secretaries, were found mostly in government.

The emergence of the modern paralegal began in the early 1980's in response to several events. First was new technology in the form of the dedicated word processor followed by the desktop computer. These produced documents much faster than the typewriter, so fewer legal secretaries were needed. Second, in the late 1970s, the U.S Supreme Court ruled that prohibition of attorney advertising was unconstitutional. This opened the door for attorney advertising, which led to competition which in turn required greater efficiency. Law firms began to create teams of attorneys and "legal assistants" (later called "paralegals"), who performed other tasks as well as document work. Today, paralegals are fully integrated into all three sectors of legal employment: private law practice, government and corporate. The role of the paralegal is especially important in civil litigation because of all the deadlines imposed by the courts.

Electronic Legal Research

One of the greatest successes with respect to the technology of law is computerized legal research. Maintaining a traditional law library is extremely expensive. Not only are the books very expensive, but so is the cost of the space to house the books. The major private electronic legal research systems in the United States are **Westlaw** and **LexisNexis**. Both systems are online subscription services that can be customized to suit the particular law firm's particular needs. Their advantages are obvious. They provide the cases, statutes and other sources of law wherever a computer can access the Internet. Both systems provide more than just access to legal authority. They also provide access to important information sources. Both systems are easy to use. The result is that law books in the process of becoming office decorations representing the past.

Electronic Filing (E-filing) In Litigation

The federal government devoted serious time and money developing electronic systems. By the late 1980's, it had developed a system for public access to federal court records that were permitted to be released known as **Public Access To Court Records or PACER**. By the late 1990's, the federal courts had an online system in place known as **Case Management/Electronic Case Files** or **CM/ECF**. As time passed, more and more of the federal courts mandated electronic filing of court documents.

In 2012, The Supreme Court of Texas, mandated that a uniform electronic filing system would be in effect in all of Texas' 254 counties and the system was completed in 2016. The system is known as **eFileTexas.Gov**. Presently, over 100 Texas counties only accept electronically filed documents in their District and County Courts.

For the most part, the e-filing systems are easy to use. E-filing is similar to sending an e-mail with an attachment. It is an economic and ecological success.

E-Discovery

The incredible expansion of the "digital universe" has led to an expansion of records that are created in the ordinary course of human activity far beyond the traditional, including e-mails, text mails, presentations in forms such as "power point," "video conference," audio and video recordings by smart phone, and so on and so forth. One thing that all of these have in common is that they may constitute evidence. The term **eDiscovery** refers to the identification, preservation, location and production of such evidence in the context of investigation and litigation. The federal court system is visibly leading the way in terms of recent changes to procedural rules. This includes more "hands on" activity by the federal trial judges in managing issues pertaining to **ESI** or **Electronically Stored Information**, beginning with rules mandating the preservation of such information. The rules are new and evolving. We will all have to stay tuned.
Conclusion

The technological challenges and innovations continue. Ethical issues ranging from storage of client information in the "cloud" to use of social media activities as evidence are all the result of technology. And the best goes on and on and on.

THANK YOU FOR READING MY BOOK

I sincerely hope you enjoyed it and your feedback online or off would be much appreciated. Feel free to also connect with me on LinkedIn. I look forward to engaging with all my readers who are interested in the "world of litigation" and wish you the very best in your endeavors.

THOMAS B. SWANSON

Thomas B. Swanson received paralegal, law enforcement, counter-terrorism and investigative training in the United States Air Force. During his initial period of training, he served as a military court bailiff and worked in military court administration. From 1973 to 1976, he was the investigator for the United States Foreign Claims Commission based in Taipei, Taiwan. While serving overseas, he investigated matters ranging from motor vehicle accidents to complex fraud and murder. In 1976, he received the **Air Force Commendation Medal** for outstanding service.

After receiving his B.A. from the University of Florida in 1978, Swanson migrated to Houston, Texas to attend law school. While in law school, he resumed conducting both criminal and civil investigations for local law firms. Swanson graduated from the South Texas College of Law and became a licensed Texas attorney in May, 1981. In 1986, he founded his own law firm. In 1988, Swanson began educating and training paralegals, which included a course in investigations. For several years during the 1980's, Swanson served as a member and vice-chairman of the Houston area Committee On Admissions, which investigated certain applicants seeking admission to the Texas bar.

As of the date of this book, Swanson has been a Texas trial lawyer for over thirty-five years. He has tried numerous civil cases in both the federal courts and the Texas state courts. In addition, he has also tried cases in the criminal courts in Texas.

For almost thirty years, Swanson has served as an instructor of paralegals in a variety of subjects, including general civil and family law litigation. He has been an invited speaker on litigation related matters to numerous groups, including a variety of professional organizations.

ABOUT THE AUTHOR

CONTACT INFO

Contact information for

THOMAS B. SWANSON
Attorney at Law

Address:

**1302 Waugh Drive, PMB 383
Houston, Texas 77019**

Phone:

(713) 447-7926

Facsimile:

(855) 422-4466

E-Mail:

velva53@hotmail.com

Made in the USA
Middletown, DE
13 May 2022

65719153R00133